Like Father—Like Sons
Created By Love...
...To Love

Paul Bersche and
Duane Levick

ISBN 978-1-63961-370-0 (paperback)
ISBN 978-1-63961-371-7 (digital)

Christian Faith Publishing
832 Park Avenue
Meadville, PA 16335
www.christianfaithpublishing.com

All biblical quotations are taken from the following translations:
Modern English Version (MEV) 2014 Edition
New American Standard Bible (NASB) 1995 Edition
New King James Version (NKJV) 1982 Edition
The Passion Translation (TPT) 2018 Edition
New International Version (NIV) 1974 Edition

All emphasis added to Scripture quotations are the author's own.

Printed in the United States of America

In loving memory of
Duane Keith Levick
1947–2021

Duane's death took place on October 20, 2021, after a long illness with lung cancer. His hope was to hold this book in his hands before he died, but God had another plan.

Duane was a Messianic Jew who loved to teach Old Testament truths and prophecies and see them fulfilled in the New Testament through the Gospel of Jesus Christ.

He loved Fatherlove!

He pressed in to *know* Him. He thought deeply about Him. He desired the fulfillment of God's dreams and visions for His church! He agonized much over an uncertain and mild-mannered church that appeared to be more accepting of the increasing influence of the "new cross" gospel, which requires nothing more than acknowledgement that God is…a modern, mediocre Christianity—part man and part god!

The Fatherlove of Duane's heart was uncompromisingly Jesus Christ, the Son of the Living God.

Paul Bersch

CONTENTS

ENDORSEMENTS

In this incredible revealing of the intention, purpose, and plan of Fatherlove, Paul Bersche and Duane Levick have assisted all of us by putting in one place a full and incredible picturesque description of what the Apostle Paul referred to as "*the mystery which for ages has been hidden in God*" (Ephesians 3:9).

Created by Love—Created to Love; Like Father—Like Sons is about the unfathomable love of God that transcends all and any earthly experience. It is about FATHERLOVE. It is about covenant. It is about the Father's purpose to have a family of His own. It is about the Father's plan to bring mature sons and daughters into a position of shared inheritance with Jesus so that together they can rule and reign in the Kingdom of God. It is not about experiencing the Father as a religious ritual or figure but in a Father-son, Father-daughter relationship built upon and surrounded by love. This book is not an "evening read," nor was it meant to be. Wrapped in Scripture, supported by prayer, and infused by the breath of the Holy Spirit, this book is an apostolic, prophetic, and teaching work as well as edifying and invigorating.

As we in the Ekklesia of this hour move closer to the fulfillment of God's purpose and plan for us and all of creation, this book, as described so clearly within its pages, allows us to have a *helicopter* view of the parade of events that took place BEFORE creation, progresses through time, and approaches the finish line at and beyond the Millennium. Questions about God's intentions with creation, the purpose of creation, and the plan for creation are answered clearly. Revelation comes as the "diary of God" (Holy Scriptures), and witness of the Holy Spirit becomes the foundation of teaching and understanding that we need to progress forward in the maturing process of sonship. What an amazing story and testimonial of Fatherlove!

Jim Sanderbeck
Overseer and President
Antioch International Ministries

What you have in your hand is a most exceptional work. At several points along the way, my heart swelled as I experienced the supreme joy of experiencing Holy Spirit revelation being unfolded in new ways. This book will make clear what God has in His mind in the creation and especially for the Godhead's crowning creation, man. The role of the Persons of the Trinity is explained and reveals Their relationship to us. You will be taken on an expeditionary tour of God's Word to reveal with elegant simplicity and clarity the vision God has for all of us to grow up into mature *sons of Love*. You will gain practical insight into how you can make the journey from being a *child* of God to that of being a *son*. The progression of the *process* of coming into all that Father has for us will inspire you to live for all that He desires for you! You will delight as the journey you are taken on leads you into the possibility of fullness in Christ. This book explains the new era God is bringing forth in time and how God is fashioning *sons* and *daughters* to inherit the *Kingdom* and rule with Christ in *eternity*.

Dr. Randy O'Dell
Senior Leader
Freedom Gateway Center

Created by Love—Created to Love Like Father—Like Sons resets your thinking regarding our purpose in the timeless plan of God. Paul Bersche and Duane Levick challenge you to rethink the pre-re-demption, pre-creation and purpose and plan of the eternal family of God. You will thoroughly enjoy this journey to embrace God the Father and His limitless love for His children, purposefully created in His image and choosing to live according to the instruction in the Word—His "diary." This is truly a well-studied, condensed reference work that can be enjoyed by serious disciples, in small group setting or educational and leadership training forums. From *predestination* to adoption, from functioning as the true *ekklesia* to how God unveils His plan to the world, you will come away from this book full of an expanded appreciation and awe of just how much you are loved by God the Father.

Senior Pastor Arthur Ledlie
Embassy

Key Endorsement

Get ready to be impacted by a theme that will touch a deep place in your heart. It is the theme of *Like Father—Like Sons*. Indeed you were *created by love—created to love*! Each chapter gave me so much to consider regarding the importance of this theme in our culture today. Brokenness abounds, often because of issues over knowing that we are loved and cherished by our Father in Heaven. I consider this book to be so significant for everyone today; every son and every father needs to read this. AND every daughter will be blessed in finding a greater love waiting for you. I hope you'll read this through carefully and consider every chapter as written just for you. May I suggest you get a copy for someone in your life, a son, or a father somewhere that needs to read this excellent book!

Brian Simmons
The Passion Translation Project

FOREWORD

As soon as my plane landed in Atlanta for a short layover, I called Duane. "Dude, this book is amazing! Every serious Christ follower needs to read this book!" On the flight from Detroit to Atlanta, I read the first half of *Created by Love—Created to Love*. It was so compelling that I read well past the point where my "air sickness from reading" kicked in!

Duane Levick and Paul Bersche are dear friends of mine, and for many years, we have been journeying into the theological realities presented in this book. During long lunch discussions, hours spent together in a house-church setting, and ministering together, these ideas not only became solid convictions; they also became solid practical ways of living in the Kingdom of Heaven on earth.

Paul and Duane embody the book they write. They both possess a deep, long-term love for God and for God's Word. They have studied it, believed it, and woven it deeply into the everyday reality of their lives. And they love people. They have used their time, gifts, and wisdom to care for and serve the people around them. I am making this point for a reason beyond just identifying they are trustworthy Christian bona fides. Paul and Duane are also solid theologians. They are learned men of the Word.

So why is this important?

Their journey into the heart of God and the Word of God has resulted in a simple understanding of the passion and plan of our Father.

That's why they write.

To make it simple.

For your benefit.

The modern church desperately needs this book.

Here's why…

First, most Christians lack a clear understanding of the heart and plan of God. Ask the average person on the street who has some basic level of faith, "What is the core teaching of Christianity?" and you will get a wide variety of answers. You will get responses from people that try to explain the whole picture by holding onto a piece or two of a puzzle.

- Love one another.
- Worship God.
- Don't sin.
- Ask Jesus into your heart.
- Take care of the unfortunate.
- Go to church.
- Keep the Ten Commandments.
- Study the Bible so it can influence your life.
- Trust God when problems arise.
- Etc., etc.,

These are all pieces of the puzzle. But none communicates the full picture of the heart and plan of God.

Without a clear picture of the big picture, "church" becomes weekly attenders who watch the professionals do the heavy lifting. Christianity is defined by church services and buildings. Faith is sequestered inside a Christian sub-culture with little expression in the public square. This feels normal to many but misses by a wide margin the impact of Christians described in the book of Acts.

The Christian community needs an extreme makeover, a revolution beginning in the hearts and minds of God's people. *Created by Love—Created to Love* exposes the identity crisis of most Christ followers and invites them into full-fledged family status allowing them to carry forward the family business.

Here's the second reason the modern church needs this book.

Society's "non-essential" assessment of today's church has a lot to do with the belief system of Christianity's leaders.

Seminaries and Bible colleges rightfully have a rigorous academic approach to understanding the realities around us. I loved the challenge of learning in this environment. But without some adjustments, it causes collateral damage. Learning about God using a philosophical/logical/academic method made God far more complicated than the God I read about in His simple story in the Bible.

God became known to me in these terms: Omniscient, Omnipresent, Omnipotent, Immutable, Sovereign, Transcendent, Immanent, Eternal, Impassible, Veracity, Trinitarian, Incomprehensibility, Impeccability, etc.,

He became an intellectual pursuit, far away and hard to know. Little capacity to really transform me.

Pastors trained in this type of system make the church primarily a classroom. Smart people win the spiritual kudos. And we've okayed marginal gains in transformation into Jesus's likeness.

Paul and Duane offer us another way! Come fall in love with a Father who created you to change the world with the power of His love.

With passionate scholarship, they paint a beautiful understanding of God's heart and plan as rooted in the Bible story. They take you on a journey into the love of God from Genesis to Revelation.

They explain the *why* questions. This makes all the difference in the world.

As your read this book, the why's of God's plan come into focus...

- The Father's love for you
- His longing for a family
- How spiritual children become powerful, world-changing, mature sons and daughter of God
- Manifesting God's Kingdom of Heaven on earth
- The shift occurring in our understanding of Ekklesia and how it changes earth
- The coming end as an incredible God-sized adventure

In my journey with Paul and Duane, my life has become a great adventure with God. I take way more Kingdom risks. I pray very differently. The way I train others has completely changed. My commitment to others is significantly deeper. Fear rarely affects me. My joy is off the charts!

From the beginning, God had a plan. *Created by Love—Created to Love* will compel you to enter the big picture of God's activities in our generation!

Senior Pastor Eric Moore
Pastor of Transformation Groups
Jubilee City Church, Detroit Region

ACKNOWLEDGMENTS

No man is an island, and there are numerous influences in our lives that contribute to who we are and what we produce. This book is the result of many things the Holy Spirit has put on our hearts over the years and many people who have crossed our path in life and have left a lasting taste of God's Glory in us.

This question that we have pursued in this work—*why did the Almighty create the world?*—was asked by the great American theologian Jonathan Edwards in 1750. It led him to write *The End for Which God Created the World,* published posthumously in 1765. Known as America's greatest theologian and the founder of the Great Awakening, Jonathan Edwards asked the same questions we asked in our "quest," and his pursuit of truth has been a blessing for us to follow in. Hopefully, we have written a present-day, simple-to-understand volume for the Ekklesia now emerging, holding true to the revelations of the Holy Spirit. Despite the difficulties of the old English writing style, our conclusions tend to be in harmony.

Another one of those special people who deeply impacted our lives was my (Paul) personal mentor, DeVern Fromke! Though DeVern is now with the Lord, my testimony of DeVern and his writings effectively influenced and encouraged Duane also.

A quiet and unassuming man, DeVern was a Christian thinker consumed with knowing God and passing on that way of seeing all of life through the eyes of the Father!

We recommend two of his classic books: *God's Ultimate Intention* and *Unto Full Stature.*

A masterful theologian, you will find some his thinking in some of the early chapters of this book.

There are two additional friends who have influenced us in this work whom we are proud to acknowledge and thank for their contributions to the Christian world. How they think, how they are consumed by both their work and their devotion to Christ, and how each has become what each write about has been an inspiration for us throughout this process.

Harold Eberle, is a brilliant Christian mind and author of over twenty books, to include the stand-alone classic *Systemic Theology of the New Apostolic Reformation* and *Christianity Unshackled*. Whether one agrees with all of Harold's conclusions or not, he creates an atmosphere of soul-searching thought, prayer, and meditation which produces clear understanding.

Brian Simmons, is the translator and commentator of The Passion Translation, a translation of Scripture that touches the "heart" of God. This life-giving truth has influenced our lives and, therefore, shows up in our book because that has become how we think!

So thank you to Brian Simmons and Harold Eberle.

We also wish to acknowledge all the multitude of believers we have been blessed to know over the years who have given us cause to study, reflect, and meditate on the Word of God in seeking out His truths, many of which are presented in this work. We look forward to joining our "family" of "sons and daughters' on "graduation day" when our Lord returns.

Finally, we want to thank our wives who have stood by us throughout this entire lengthy process, supporting us, being resonate sounding boards and spiritual warriors as we battled the up and down year of 2020 in writing this book.

My (Paul) personal thanks to Carolyn who has stood by me for sixty-four years in marriage and ministry as the family intercessor, and my (Duane) personal thanks to Grace, a true woman of God who lives and walks with Him 24/7. Anyone on a "mission," in our case writing this book, knows the value and the blessing of having God-fearing, praying wives to stand by them and support them.

We also wish to thank you, the reader, for without you, this is only so much paper.

INTRODUCTION

Back in the 2000s, it became popular to use the prefix *dis* as a slang word of its own accord. Spoken as *dis, dissed,* or *dissing,* it came to mean being *insulted, disrespected,* and *put down; to find fault with;* or *speak ill of.* During the past forty years, Christianity has been increasingly *dissed* as being *outdated, anti-society, and anti-science.* Compromise and inclusiveness is the "new normal" *acceptance of the religion of Christianity,* while true believers are *dissed* as being primitive, steeped in bigotry, and even branded as right-wing terrorists. But those brands do not replace or change the plan that the FATHER originally put in place.

God is the same yesterday, today, and forever. **People change— God does not.**

When used as intended, the prefix means to "*do the opposite of; to expel;* or *to be separate from.*" For example, the word *displeasure* means "*to have the opposite of pleasure*"—*pleasure* meaning *enjoyment* and *dis* meaning "*to separate from,*" so the word *displeasure means being separated from enjoyment.*

Our nation, the world, is in a condition of ***dis—disease***—not only *disease* from a pandemic but a ***disease* of *separation*** from the FATHER Creator. *Dis (separate from) ease (comfort, rest, peace)*—meaning we are in a state of *separation from comfort, rest, and peace.* We are ***diseased***—*from our Creator, and people are suffering as a result.* Only God can provide us with *real* rest and peace. The LOVE of our FATHER created us to live under His rest and peace. But we are attempting to live on our own *self-love,* rejecting the LOVE of the FATHER. We are not made to exist like that. Rejecting our FATHER'S LOVE results in **dis-ease**. Separation from GOD means separation from peace. God is light, so when we live in separation from God, we exist in separation from light—in other words, we exist in darkness. If we continue to exist in that condition, we will go into eternity in that condition, and we will inherit eternal darkness and separation from our FATHER. That is not what the Creator intended or desires of us.

The objective of this book is to show and express what God's purpose is, not as we *interpret* it or to *develop* a doctrine around it but as THE FATHER intended it and revealed it in His Holy Word. What God intended for humankind was revealed over two thousand years ago. It has been there all along. So much of Christianity did not see it, mainly because they were not looking for it.

We have gotten sidetracked—distracted—away from the lofty and marvelous plan and purpose God had originally placed us on a path to obtain because we had it all wrong. We are not here for our purposes and our will. It is not about me. It is all about HIM— our LORD—Jesus Christ, and about the FATHER's great LOVE. God LOVES HIS SON and GOD LOVES US and HE created and put a plan in motion that gives joy, happiness, and shalom to HIMSELF, the SON, the HOLY SPIRIT, and to all who will accept.

Within the pages of this book, we will unveil to you, brick by brick, God's *Ultimate Intention, Purpose, and Plan with Creation* and LIFE, what the Apostle Paul called the "*mystery*" hidden through the ages.

This book is the "medicine" to show how to cure the "<u>dis</u>-ease" of separation from our FATHER.

Christians learn a lot about the world, America, church, and ourselves during the times of crisis and worldwide panic. When the world does not know or understand the events sweeping across the globe, believers in Jesus Christ may not know the answers any better, but we find great comfort and solace in resting in the peace of Almighty God. There, we not only find calmness and grace, but the Holy Spirit imparts understanding and revelation regarding the "*things of God.*" And we know this is all *temporal* and will pass, so we have to, as the Apostle Paul said,

> *be cheerful with joyous celebration in every*
> *season of life. Let joy overflow, for you are united*
> *with the Anointed One!... Don't be pulled in differ-*

ent directions or worried about a thing. Be saturated in prayer throughout each day—then God's wonderful peace that transcends human understanding will make the answers known to you through Jesus Christ. (Philippians 4:4–9 TPT)

The current timing for this book is more pertinent than ever! Across the globe, there is a clear attack on fatherhood. Fatherhood is downplayed, underrated, and ridiculed, even to the point of the natural male gender identity being challenged, dismissed, and medically altered. The very laws of life and nature that God laid out are being viciously and defiantly brushed aside like so much societal trash. The results are crime, suicide, depression, and drug dependency rates increasing at unprecedented levels, as well as a wave of coldhearted lawlessness, lacking in compassion sweeping across the land and the world. Add to that, we are creating a generation that is totally confused about who and what they are! This generation is next in line to "rule" the world. If that does not concern you, then nothing will.

The absence of fatherhood within our country at every level—family fathers, church fathers, national fathers, spiritual fathers, and natural fathers—is a major contributing factor to the unrest, upheaval, depression, and evil that has erupted across our nation and world. There is an enemy to God and goodness, and he knows that family and fatherhood are what God desires, so he is waging an all-out war against both.

And **Fatherhood** is what this book is all about.

When trouble comes, children go to their mothers for comfort. Sons go to their fathers for advice and counsel. We are God's sons; trouble has come, and we cry out, *"Abba Father!"*

And that is why this book is written. God desires that none should perish but that ALL should come to HIM—the FATHER—not in a ritual, religious, man-centered way but in a FATHER-SON, FATHER-DAUGHTER relationship built upon and surrounded in LOVE.

Immediately, we become acutely aware that our relationship with God needs a touch-up or, more likely, a complete overhaul.

Everything around us needs His urgent attention! We need God's intervention into our society—our life, our nation, our world!

With that said, the message of this book does not flow out of a crisis mentality! This book flows out of the church's complacency—its lethargic, noncommittal, humanistic mentality. Historically, the church in America has had a rich and powerful influence on American society and culture, but today, the church has been fast asleep for many years. It has become focused on *earthly* issues rather than the Kingdom-of-God issues. Today's church exists in a Christian-looking facade of human-oriented self-help social programs rather than LIFE-**changing transformation**. The church today is more interested in entertainment than worship! Entertainment, social programs, prosperity, and Bible compromise have become our religion. Like the church at Ephesus, we have lost our first love.

This whole new mix of philosophy to appease this unique style of Christianity has come from one fundamental flaw: we have lost the AWE of FATHER GOD. It is in that mystical AWE that we find the majesty of God—the *Greatness* and *Magnificence* of God, Creator of all things, God of light, Father of all, the awe, the glory, the majesty of God, the *high and lifted-up* God, above all things, above all people, places, and times. Where has that **awe** gone?

The moment that AWE began to fade and move to the *back burners* of our spirits and souls was the moment we began a downward spiral. We went from God-centered to self-centered, rationalizing it with good deeds, social awareness, inclusiveness, and moral compromise.

It seems the natural family images of father, mother, father-son, father-daughter have been disqualified and dismissed by our present cultural patterns as unnecessary for living life with meaningful and fulfilling purpose. "*It takes a village*" is the new mantra that has replaced FATHERHOOD. This new lifestyle is constantly adjusting downward to a more culturally friendly God, one that is *socially* acceptable, one that is permissive in all things and whose only concern with us is that we have all the "things" we think we should have to make us happy. We have molded God into a combination of Santa

Claus and the Jolly Green Giant. As such, *God* loses His AWE and becomes a reflection of what men want Him to be.

The question this book asks is, **is this what God intended when He first made creation? If not, then what did HE intend?**

This book will attempt to show God's *original intention, purpose, and plan* with creation, church, and people by unwrapping the *when, what,* and *why* of God's creation.

That final question is a burning question for you—the reader. On a personal note, *"Why do I care? Why study it? Why even consider it?"*

The answer is simple: because God did "it," and this "it" is our creation—our existence. Without "it," we do not exist. God created us in His image, and our spirits yearn for and seek our Creator. It is God's very breath that gives us *life*. We cry out to our Creator, seeking to know Him and relate to Him. And we ask the question, *what does my Creator want from me? Am I fulfilling His purpose in creating me?*

By knowing His purpose, we know our purpose; by knowing our purpose, WE **exist with purpose**.

No matter what you believe or do not believe regarding the future history of the world and where we stand regarding God's overall plan for life on this planet, one thing everyone can agree on: something is happening! It has begun, and it is not going to stop. Something is going down—something big and something world changing. Everyone with *"eyes to see and ears to hear"* knows there is more to come.

The church is the only thing standing in the way of evil! It is time for it to wake up and understand its purpose and destiny—and to grab hold of it! *Our Ultimate Purpose is to worship, praise, and honor our Creator.*

We welcome you to come along and join us on this journey, back to the very beginning of all things, starting with a private "council" meeting that occurred *before the foundations of the world were laid.*

Welcome aboard! Sit back and enjoy the journey.

A NOTE ABOUT THE BOOK

Some of our methods in writing this book are a little different than the norm. If that is a hindrance for you, we apologize for that. It is not our intention to distract you but rather to emphasize various points, ideas, and concepts for your consideration and meditation.

You will notice an abundance of Scripture is used and quoted in the text instead of being referenced to look up. This is deliberate in maintaining the integrity of God's Word and because the Scriptures quoted flow naturally with the text of the book and should be read as part of the text. Please **do not skip over them** but read them, knowing that the Holy Spirit is the real author of this book, and those are His Words.

We are excited that you have chosen to read this book. Our prayer is that it blesses you in reading and studying it as it has blessed us in writing it. The Holy Spirit has been our leader and teacher with the writing. May HE be your leader and teacher with the reading.

CHAPTER 1

THE GREAT "BEFORE"

Come with me on a journey in time…

    —flip back the pages of history…past the millenniums of humankind…back beyond the existence of all things…back further still… back to when there were no *things*—no material, no atmosphere—back to before the *"In the Beginning…"*

Back to the *"Great Before."*

    Before trees and leaves…

      before rivers and seas…

        before planets…and moons

          galaxies and stars.

Back before there was a universe…

    before things were measured by days

    and years and millenniums.

Journey back in time to a time when…

    there was no time.

      Back before there was…anything.

Yes…back to the time when there was nothing…when there was only void…nothing…

    —nothing except a blinding, *unapproachable light.*

He alone has immortality, dwelling in unapproachable light, whom no man has seen or can see, to whom be honor and everlasting power. (1 Timothy 6:16 NASB)

The Triune God—*Father, Son, Holy Spirit*—existing as one, united in joy, awash in light and love.

We know God existed in perfect harmony within Himself, a "*council*" of three, the TRINITY—FATHER, SON, and HOLY SPIRIT. Like a deep, heavy surf, rolling and surging with omniscient whitecaps of light, Their love rolled and washed over each other. It flowed back and forth, an endless sea of waves of immeasurable joy, contentment, and peace—*Shalom Peace*. They were each separate, yet together. They were one, and They knew no evil, no jealousies of one another, only goodness and love.

God is good, and His love has no boundaries. His love flows without limits or obstructions. It holds no ill thoughts, carries no false perceptions, is pure, unblemished. God does not possess Love—God IS love, and this borderless, boundless love is the magnificence of Their *glory* that They held and shared together.

So, my Father, restore me back to the glory that we shared together when we were face-to-face before the universe was created. (John 17:5 TPT)

Yes, before anything existed, They shared their love with one another. They each had a voice, were a *council* of Three, yet united as one, sharing "*the glory*" of Their love for one another, face-to-face, *before the universe was created.* Waves of light swept over and through the Son and the FATHER, creating a radiant bond of *glory* beyond anything that humankind can imagine or experience.

Love is the *glory* of God—*glory* is the visible and felt manifestation of FATHER'S LOVE. It pulsated at the seams of Their consciousness, eager to burst forth. In the existence of nothingness, They were a radiant, boundless love-light, pulsing and radiating Their power, magnificence, and glory.

Those who are loved by God, let his love continually pour from you to one another because God is love. Everyone who loves is fathered by God. (1 John 4:7–10 TPT)

Unapproachable in its power, vibrant in its pureness, splendid in its greatness, unmeasurable in its *glory*, exalted in its magnificence, God existed as Love.

In our feeble and primitive minds, we ask the obvious, *where did God come from?*

We do not know—and probably never will. Such things are beyond our ability to know, and it is just as well. Some things…we just do not need to know.

We know He was—and we know He is—because our *spirits* cry out to Him and resonate with Him. He is our FATHER, and that is enough for us to know.

Then amid the swells of LOVE washing over them, the Father had a new thought. He desired to reach outward—to extend, to share the goodness, the glory, the beauty of His love.

An unspoken thought floated in a wave across the council of three:

Expand the glory.
    Share the Love. The reply resonated back.
        Yes—expand the Glory! Share the Love!
The council was in harmonic agreement.
        With what do we share?
        With things—material things—let us create material things.
            Yes, Father! Visible, touchable things.
            A universe.
            Galaxies.
                Stars.
                    A world.
        With trees.
            Animals.
                And people.

People—after our image—people to share with.
Yes, people to share the glory of love with.
Sons to share the glory of love with.
A Kingdom.
A Kingdom of light and love.
A Kingdom of people.
A Kingdom of sons and daughters.
A Kingdom of love.
Yes, Father—let it be so—let us create.
Just speak the Word, My Son.
Yes, Father, I will speak.
"Let there be."

CHAPTER 2

IN THE BEGINNING

And so…God CREATED.

He spoke the *WORD*.

And a universe came into existence:

> Galaxies, supernovas, solar systems, planets, and moons seemingly without end, sprang forth and filled the emptiness. Billions of stars and suns, too numerous to comprehend, filled the void of nothingness and continues to expand outward even to this day.

God experienced creativity:

> Molecules formed, chemical and electrical processes came into existence and began interacting one with another, each independent and stand-alone, yet dependent on the others to sustain life. Trees, leaves, and flowers sprang forth. Fish and birds of various shapes, sizes, and designs began to swim and fly. Animals and creatures, from the smallest ladybug to the towering brontosaurus, came into existence, moving across the earth, feeling the ground beneath them for the very first time. The world teemed and overflowed with life.

And God enjoyed His creativity:

> In addition to sharing His goodness and LOVE, creation afforded God the occasion to indulge in an artistic explosion that put His power, wisdom, and imagination on display. With His creation, God gave Himself free rein to indulge in all His creative

and artistic skills. The vastness, complexity, and yet unparalleled simplicities of creation are light-years beyond our ability to understand and grasp. We can only stand in awe and wonder at the awesomeness of a thunderstorm or the majesty of a sunrise, stare in amazement at the complexities of the human anatomy, the astonishing thinking ability of the brain, or absorb the hypnotic rhythms of the oceans' surf. Within the breathtaking beauty of all that God created, from the tiniest leaf of the smallest shrub to the giant redwoods reaching upward to over three hundred feet proclaiming their glory, a never-ending amazement staggers our consciousness, witnessing to the power, beauty, and greatness of the Creator.

> *The heavens declare the glory of God, and the firmament shows His handiwork.* (Psalm 19:1 NKJV)

> *Lift up your eyes on high, And see who has created these things, Who brings out their host by number; He calls them all by name, By the greatness of His might And the strength of His power; Not one is missing.* (Isaiah 40:26 NKJV)

> *O Lord, how manifold are Your works! With wisdom You have made them all; the earth is full of Your creatures.* (Psalm 104:24 NKJV)

> *Sing and shout with passion; make a spectacular sound of joy—For God's Word is something to sing about! He is true to his promises, his word can be trusted, and everything he does is reliable and right. The Lord loves seeing justice on the earth. Anywhere and everywhere, you can find his faithful, unfailing love! All he had to do was speak by his Spirit-wind command, and God created the heavenlies. Filled with galaxies and stars, the vast*

*cosmos he wonderfully made. His voice scooped out
the seas. The ocean depths he poured into vast reser-
voirs. Now, with breathtaking wonder, let everyone
worship Yahweh, this awe-inspiring Creator. Words
he breathed and worlds were birthed. "Let there be,"
and there it was—Springing forth the moment he
spoke. No sooner said than done!* (Psalm 33:1–9
TPT)

You can almost see God laughing, relishing in all the colors,
sounds, and smells He created. HE was the *master painter*, the *prod-
igy composer*, the *elite tester*, and the *connoisseur taster* of the *greatest
masterpiece* ever imagined. His power, knowledge, artistic beauty, and
wisdom were bursting forth at the seams as He created the heavens
and the earth.

*In the beginning, I was there, for God possessed
me even before he created the universe… Before the
oceans depths were poured out, and before there were
any glorious fountains overflowing with water, I was
there, dancing! Even before one mountain had been
sculpted or one hill raised up, I was already there,
dancing! When he created the earth, the fields, even
the first atom of dust, I was already there. When
he hung the tapestry of the heavens and stretched
out the horizon of the earth, when the clouds and
skies were set in place and the subterranean fountains began to flow strong, I was already there. when
he set in place the pillars of the earth and spoke the
decrees of the seas, commanding the waves so that
they would not overstep their boundaries, I was
there, close to the Creator's side as his master artist.
Daily he was filled with delight in me as I playfully
rejoiced before him. I laughed and played, so happy
with what he had made, while finding my delight
in the children of men.* (Proverbs 8:22–31 TPT)

In His rebuke of Job, God showed His enjoyment with creating. We feel His pleasure, His overflowing love and happiness with the intricacies of His creation. He is overcome with the beauty, the complexities, and the majesty of what He has done. Almost as if bragging to Job:

> *Where were you when I laid the foundations of the earth? Declare, if you have understanding. Who has determined its measurements if you know? Or who has stretched the line upon it? To what are its foundations fastened? Or who laid its cornerstone when the morning stars sang together, and all the sons of God shouted for joy?* (Job 38:4–7 NKJV)

> *Have you entered the treasuries of the snow? Or have you seen the treasuries of the hail? By what way is the light diffused, or the east wind scattered upon the earth?… Does the rain have a father? Or who has produced the drops of dew? From whose womb came the ice? And the frost of heaven, who gives it birth?… Can you tie the cords to the Pleiades or loosen the belt of Orion? Can you bring out the constellation in its season? Or can you guide the Bear with its cubs? Do you know the ordinances of heaven? Can you lift up your voice to the clouds, that abundance of waters may cover you? Can you send lightning that they may go forth and say to you, "Here we are"?… Do you know the time when the wild mountain goats produce offspring? Or can you observe when the deer gives birth?… Did you give the beautiful wings to the peacocks? Or wings and feathers to the ostrich? Have you given the horse strength? Have you clothed his neck with thunder?… Does the hawk fly by your wisdom, and stretch her wings toward the south? Does the eagle mount up at*

your command and make her nest on high? (Job 38,
39 NKJV, abbreviated)

He created prisms of colors, symphonies of sounds, bouquets
of scents, and a cornucopia of tastes, all bordered in a panorama
of beauty and glory. He created the five senses for living creatures,
enabling them to interact and enjoy one another by hearing, seeing,
touching, smelling, and tasting the created life around them—each
sense bringing discovery and glorification to His creation and God.

And God created man and woman, molding and shaping them
with His own hands and breathing life into them with His own
breath. He endowed them with all five of the physical senses, providing them with the maximum means to enjoy His creation to the
fullest in all ways possible.

God was pleased with His creation.

And all that He made…was *"good."*

Why Creation?

What was God's intention when He created the universe? What
was the desire of His heart when He first spoke material things into
existence? When only He existed as the Triune God, the Trinity—
Father, Son, and Holy Spirit—joined in accord, awash in glory, and
united in love, what drove Him to move beyond His horizon and to
create new?

What was His intention when He created man and woman?

When someone loves something, they want, more than ever, to
share that something and that love with others. We want people to
know and feel the goodness we know and feel. God is no different.
He loves His *goodness*, and He wants to *share* it, *expand* it, *glorify* it…
with others.

We think we understand the story of man, but we do not understand the story of God. We know the *how* of creation, but do we
know the *why?* Maybe if we could understand the story of God just a
little bit better, we would understand the *why—just a little bit better*.
And maybe that would help us to understand the story of man—*just*

a little bit better. And maybe then we could fulfill God's *purpose* He has for us—*just a little bit better*.

A Mad Scientist

In 1818, a teenage English girl named Mary Shelley, on an overnight challenge, penned a novel titled *Frankenstein; or, the Modern Prometheus*.[1] It was the story of a mad scientist, Victor Frankenstein, who created a *living* being from an assortment of dead body parts and some jolts of electricity. While not written as such, the book was Doctor Frankenstein's *diary* of his interaction and relationship with his *creation*. For him, the *Ultimate Purpose* of his *creation* was to prove he could do it.

It is a sad story of a creature created in a charged atmosphere of snapping, sizzling bolts of electricity and bellowing thunder—but void of love. In the novel, Victor abandons his *creation* and regrets making him. The creature finds Victor's *diary* and reading it leaves him with anger, remorse, and bitterness at being *created*, along with a thirst for revenge against his creator.

Frankenstein is the embodiment of *living flesh* that processes a *troubled soul* and *lacks his father's* love.

The God of creation is not a *mad* scientist, and He did not create the universe to prove He could do it. He does not need to *prove* He can *create* life—HE IS LIFE—and HE did not need snapping, sizzling bolts of electricity and peals of cascading thunder (or old dead body parts for that matter) to create, not only man but the entire universe. He created all of them—the electricity, the peals of thunder, and not only body *parts* but *new living bodies*—by just speaking the *words*, and it was so, the power and majesty of God revealed! HE existed in total contentment and peace, as the Triune God, having no need to *prove* anything.

And He did not *regret* making man—at least not at this stage. Later, after some unwanted *supernatural* intervention, God had a moment of regret. But that is another story.

---
[1] https://en.wikipedia.org/wiki/Frankenstein.

"In the beginning—God..." begins the process of revealing God's story of creation. And that is enough for us to start with. God is—period! We do not need to understand it. We accept it.

Why accept it? Because it makes the most sense of anything, and our spirits resonate with it. Here is our simple answer to the question of God's existence.

Material things exist—that is a fact without dispute. We all agree with that premise. We see *material* things. We touch *material* things. We live with *material* things. We are smothered in a world of *material* things. Our entire lives consist of a long procession of collecting *material* things that we sort through, buy, sell, hoard, and discard. We exist as *material* things.

Well, if *material* things exist—and we all agree they do—then by logical certainty, *material thing creators must* exist also. You cannot have one without the other. Think about anything, your car, for example. Your car exists. It sits in your driveway. You see it, you touch it, you wash it, and you drive it. It is there—you enjoy it, and you use it. But it did not just suddenly materialize out of nowhere from nothing. It is there because of a car *creator*. In this case, many *creators*—engineers who designed it; steelworkers who made the steel; rubber makers who made the tires; electronic engineers, designers, and technicians who designed and built all the controls and safety devices; and the assemblers who put all the parts together in the proper order; not to talk about the haulers and dealers who made it available. There are hundreds of people (*creators)* involved in putting your car in your driveway. You would laugh at anyone who suggested to you that your car just suddenly appeared out of nowhere or that it *created* and *made* itself out of nothing. It exists because car *creators* existed first.

Likewise, it is just as absurd to look at the universe and say it just *appeared* out of nowhere all by itself—on its own. Galaxies, solar systems, stars, suns, planets, space itself; water, land, trees, flora, birds, animals, and fish—all the intricacies that go into each one, each dependent on the other for survival—to assume that they all just *appeared* out of nowhere ON THEIR OWN is the height of foolishness. They exist—we see them, we touch them, we live with them—

therefore, somewhere a *Creator* exists, a *Creator* who is far beyond human understanding, capability, knowledge, wisdom, and power. We may not understand it, but creation shouts it—and our hearts sing it! We grasp it, we accept it, and we move on with it! It is a foundational stone that we receive to begin building on. It takes more *faith* to believe that the universe's material things somehow materialized by themselves out of nothing than it does to believe in a Creator. I do not have to understand God to believe in His existence. I am surrounded by many things I do not understand, yet they are there in front of me. I would have to deny all my senses and logic to accept such reasoning.

There are many reasons beyond creation for believing in a supernatural God, and if the reader desires or needs to pursue this, I suggest the reader check out a good "apologetic" work such as Josh McDowell's *God-Breathed* or Lee Strobel's *The Case for God.*

So that brings us back to our original question of *"Why?"*

This IS a legitimate question for us to ask: *Why DID God create things? Why DID He "speak" all of creation into existence? Why DID God form and create man—in His image? What was in the heart of God that spurred Him on when He had all He needed?*

Did He have a purpose? *If so, what was His purpose?*

Some shrug and ask, *"Does it matter? God created us, and here we are. What does it matter why? Just be glad you're alive. Live your life and be content."*

That may work for some, but ultimately, not knowing God's purpose in creating us leaves our life *without purpose.* How can we be *content* if we are missing the *purpose* of our existence? If I am a *created* being, I want to know my *Creator* and *why* HE created me.

Man has been striving to find the answer to that question since breath first inflated his lungs. A yearning and rumbling deep within our spirits reaches out and seeks its Creator. Our spirits and our souls cry out to know what their true purpose is. This empty chamber in our hearts is what separates us from the rest of all creation.

Like Mary Shelley's "creature," knowing the answer may make us angry and bitter. But seeing the beauty of God's creation all around us, our spirits say, *"No, there will be no anger, no bitterness. God is love, and all things have been created in beauty and love, so proceed. Seek and find the answer."*

So to our question:

"Does it matter?"

"Yes, it matters!"

Embarking on the Quest

Our quest then, within these pages, is to find the answer to the *"Why?"* Not the small *whys* of life. There is no shortage of books out there telling us all about the *why's* of life and how to avoid them, fight them, run from them, embrace them, ignore them—or do whatever you want to do with them! No, we are going on a *big-game* hunt. We are going after the big *"WHY?"* Why did God undertake this whole plan of creation and everything that has transpired since? What was (is) He trying to do? And therefore, what is it that He is expecting from His creation—us? What was God's intention in the beginning, and what is His intention today? In other words,

Why do you and I exist?

For certain, we cannot have the full understanding of who God is. Such knowledge is beyond our comprehension, and such a question is *not* a legitimate question for the *creation* to ask of the Creator. But wouldn't it be nice if God had left a *diary* of His *creation* so we, like Victor Frankenstein's creature, could find it and see what answers, if any, it held for ourselves?

Well, turns out, He did.

It is the Bible—the Holy Scriptures—consisting of sixty-six separate writings by more than forty different authors from different cultures, eras, and generations, covering more than 1,500 years, that all fit and converge together into God's *Diary* of His interaction with His creation. Inspired by the Holy Spirit, the Bible gives us insight into the Creator's mind and heart. It provides us with great insight into the character and nature of God. No, it does not tell us *who* God is, but it tells us *what* God is. *God is Life...God is light...God is Love...God is Good...God is the All-knowing and Almighty.*

Those who are loved by God, let his love continually pour from you to one another because God is love. Everyone who loves is fathered by God and experiences an intimate knowledge of him. The one who does not love has yet to know God, for God is love. The light of God's love shined within us when he sent his matchless Son into the world so that we might live through him. This is love: He loved us long before we loved him. It was his love, not ours. (1 John 4:7–10 TPT)

We are not created from leftover body parts like Victor Frankenstein's *creation* was. We are created *"In the Image"* of God Himself, and the knowledge of our creation does not leave us with anger, bitterness, or a thirst for revenge like his *creation* held. Instead, we are filled with thankfulness, praise, and love for our Creator. We seek to know our Creator more intimately. We strive to know what His *Intention and Purpose* was in creating us.

Being created by LOVE, from LOVE, and for LOVE, we seek to know our FATHER'S LOVE.

Over the centuries, our attempt to explore God and man's relationship has resulted in numerous belief systems and theologies. Looking across the spectrum of these religious systems, we ask ourselves, *have these beliefs tapped into the heart and intention of God?*

Most do not attempt it. They focus on the outward manifestations of God, maintaining a hands-off approach as to the *why*. The storm comes, the rain falls, the lightning flashes, the thunder rolls. Primitive man huddles in fear and seeks an understanding of the storm. In time, he learns the *how's* of rain, lightning, and thunder, but does he know the *why's* of the storm? *"The gods did it."* And that is sufficient—for a season. But then he learns the "things" of the weather—cold fronts, pressure inversions, cloud formations, and rain cycles. And by learning these things, he understands the *why* of the storm, and the next time the storm comes, he does not huddle in fear from the thunder and lightning. He understands it, and by understanding it, he embraces it.

So it is with our journey with God who openly shares His personal *Diary* with us. If He shared in His *Diary* the *why* of creation, we can learn and understand. And by understanding, we can embrace creation with the lustiness of life that maybe God intended us to have from the beginning.

If the Creator *wants us to know* what His purpose and desire was with *creation*, His *Diary* will hold the answers. With that as our foundation, everything we do on this quest will be solely referenced, supported, and presented through God's *Diary*—the *Holy Scriptures*. No human-based theories or ideas will be offered unless clearly labeled as such, only what the *Word of God* reveals to us and the Holy Spirit confirms will we consider. (*Look on the bright side. If revelation is forthcoming, we will learn our purpose. If revelation is not forthcoming, then this will be a very short book. Either way, you cannot go wrong.*)

Are you ready? Okay.

Let's go.

CHAPTER 3

THE STARTING PLACE

So far, we have established that God is *Creator,* and we are *creation.* Where do we go from here? Since we are looking into the questions surrounding *creation,* it would seem a logical place to begin looking would be *creation.*

God as Creator and us as *creation* establishes a *hierarchy.* Is our relationship with our Creator only to be a hierarchy? For the majority of religions, the answer is *yes.* The gods are on one level, and humans are on another level and never shall the twain meet, unless man has done something to anger the gods, in which case there will be punishment. (It is amazing how many Christians believe that very same logic regarding Christianity.)

Creation as the Starting Place

Well, we do not have to go and anger the gods. We have the *Diary*—the Words of the Creator. Does the *Diary* say anything about it? It does.

In fact, the first three chapters of the opening *book* of the *Diary* (Genesis 1–3) talk about it in detail. The exact sequence may not be crystal clear, but all the pertinent background and facts are there:

- God "*spoke*" everything into existence—except for man whom He personally formed from the earth.

- God made man in His *own* image. He did that for nothing else in creation.
- God breathed His breath into man to give him life.
- God made woman to be a companion to man and complete the *family* concept.
- God placed them in a beautiful garden He created.
- God gave them dominion over all creation.
- God fellowshipped with them.

These actions demonstrate a relationship that goes beyond hierarchy. They show a personal involvement of the Creator with *humankind* creation. It is clear by God's actions that our relationship to the Creator was to be more than hierarchical. (*You cannot get much more personal than having one's breath giving life to another.*)

To understand what that relationship is, we must know what the Creator's intention was—from the beginning.

And immediately, we have a problem: these chapters tell us the *what*, *where*, and *how* of creation, but they don't tell us the *why* of creation. They do not tell what God's intention was.

We learn one important thing from these passages—God did not desire to have *mindless robots* to fellowship with. His garden included a *no-trespassing* zone, along with instructions *not* to eat of a certain tree which was *"good for food, that it was pleasing to the eyes and a tree desirable to make one wise."* By that statement, it is clear this tree was a temptation. It is also clear that God wanted fellowship with people who would *voluntarily* follow His instructions despite temptation.

Continue reading in the *Diary*, and we learn that early on, after the *"In the beginning,"* man messed up and did NOT follow God's instructions regarding that tree. At this point in our quest, because the search focuses on *human purpose*, we get easily diverted off the main track onto a side spur. We were on the right path to unveiling God's *Ultimate Intention*, but we got derailed by getting distracted.

"Distracted? Distracted by what?"

"Not by what but by whom."

"Whom? Who is that?"

"Adam."

"Adam? You do not mean the Adam in the..."

"Yes, I mean the Adam in the garden."

Adam distracted us by shifting the focus from God and creation to himself and his failure. The disobedience in the garden has resulted in our *preoccupation with sin and with Adam's disobedience*, which has distracted us from looking deeper into God's original purpose. We call it the *Fall*, and it is forever stamped on our minds so that it *overshadows and dominates all our thoughts regarding God's ultimate intention.* Now understand, it is not that the *Fall* and its resultant redemption are not significant. They most certainly are, and *thank God for His redemption. Without it, game over!*

But the Fall and man's redemption are not the story of God's original purpose. They are not even the core of the story, nor are they the end or the beginning of the story. Together, they are but one part of the story, one giant detour within the story. *An essential detour for sure, for without it, we are lost!* But a detour all the same. And those pictures engraved forever in our minds of the two *"fallen"* humans being expulsed from the garden have caused us to forget that we have not yet uncovered God's *Original Purpose* for creation.

Beginning at creation as the *starting place* of our quest results in a *God-centered* scenario because creation is all about God, and *man* does not enter the picture until the last day of creation. That is the good part. But when he does, the relationship deteriorates and reverts again to a *man-to-God* relationship from man's viewpoint. God creates man...man serves God...man sins...God redeems man. As such, it remains focused on *man's* shortcomings and actions. That is the bad part.

This cannot be the full story! Scripture does not say, *"In the beginning was man, and man created God so that he could be forgiven of his failures."*

Let us look at what the *Diary* does say about God's original plan of creation:

> Then God said, "Let us make man in our
> image, after our likeness, and let them have domin-

ion over the fish of the sea, and over the birds of the air, and the livestock, and over all the earth, and over every creeping thing that creeps on the earth." So, God created man in His own image; in the image of God, He created him; male and female He created them. (Genesis 1:26–27 MEV)

Then the Lord God formed man from the dust of the ground and breathed into his nostrils the breath of life, and man became a living being. The Lord God planted a garden in the east, in Eden, and there He placed the man whom He had formed… And the Lord God commanded the man, saying, "Of every tree of the garden you may freely eat, but of the tree of the knowledge of good and evil you shall not eat, for in the day that you eat from it you will surely die." (Genesis 2:7–9 MEV)

These tell us *what*. They do not tell us *why*.

Creation as the Starting Place in our quest will not work. We need to find another place.

The Fall as the Starting Place

God created a material world and gave it to man to manage. God shared His *creation* with man, whom He created in His own image and breathed His life-giving breath into.

Adam was given a choice—to stay on the path that God planned or not. He *"fell"* off the path and chose his own way, and the human race followed him into blindness!

From that day forward, *man has been the focus of man.* Because of the consequences of the *Fall,* our focus shifted to how do we overcome it? How do we get back into the *good graces* of our Creator? And of course, the answer is we do not do anything—except believe in God's Son as our Redeemer. It is all by God's grace and LOVE that we are *reinstated* back into His original *Plan* with nothing more on our part than forgiveness.

And that is a marvelous, wonderful gift that our Creator has given us, so glorious and wonderful that, for most, we cannot seem to move beyond it. We get hung up on our good fortune and tend to *hang out* at salvation and redemption. While on the surface that is a good thing, in the long run, we must ask, *am I fulfilling God's Original Purpose and Plan for myself?"*

If man comes to the Lord only to be saved, then follow the logic: man's purpose in God's plan is to sin so to be restored and redeemed. That logically leads us to believe God's intention is that man's *ultimate purpose is to fail and fall* so to be *redeemed!*

What then do we conclude is God's purpose? To *forgive* and *redeem?* Can that be it? God created ALL of creation so that He can spend eternity forgiving and saving us? Where is there any ultimate purpose in that scenario? Where is the lost *glory* the Son gave up reclaimed in that?

When we seek to understand the purpose from the point where man "Falls," then *man takes center stage and overshadows the story of God*, and we must always remember, this is not *man's* story; it is *God's* story. Where you go to church—how you worship, how you pray—what you understand about the ways and the truth of God are then all based on sin, forgiveness, and redemption. The concept is that man appeared on the stage of time just for the sole purpose of salvation as if God needed to justify the need to have Himself in His own scenario, so he created man to validate His own existence by having to redeem him. Convoluted logic at best, completely faulty at its core.

Man then becomes important to God's purpose only in his failures. When man fails, he recognizes his failure and comes to God to be redeemed. God's chief work then is seen as redemptive. What is our assignment on earth? *To sin, of course—so to be redeemed!* And that leads us to justify sinning—*"I'm only human, and it's natural for me to sin. Besides, God will forgive me."* Or taking it to the extreme—*"God needs me to sin to justify His existence."* This cannot be.

All this effort and focus is done to *validate God's position* of being *God—the Redeemer*, with His sole intent to redeem humankind. We have hijacked God's original purpose by creating a whole religion based on the *Fall* alone, without yet knowing or understanding anything about God's original purpose or intent with creation from the very beginning.

Throughout our Christian walk, we embrace that theme continually, being restored and reconciled to God over and over again and again. We have revival meetings in the spring and again in the fall, and we respond to BOTH altar calls so that we can continually maintain our *highest level of being restored by His redemptive grace.* Logically, this concludes that man should continue to *sin* so that he always needs to be *restored*, and God can attain His fullest measure of purpose by eternally being the *great Redeemer.*

And so we keep preaching and calling for seasoned believers *(backsliders)* to be revived and restored. And they are *restored* repeatedly, getting "saved" repeatedly at altar call after altar call. Can this possibly be the purpose God had planned out? And is this true *transformation?*

To this day, man is always on man's mind—preoccupied with himself, his needs, his desires, his well-being. Man sees everything from man's viewpoint. All thought of God is dominated by *man-centeredness!* Even when we turn to God, all too often, the *true* focus in our turning is not God but ourselves and what can God do for us today.

This can cause us to be pleased with ourselves by being "redeemed," and then a level of self-righteous arrogance can set in, thinking we are above others. We think waving our redemption around like a red flag is what God is all about when in fact, the whole thing is sinning against God because all along, we have not recognized that it is not about us but Him and *His glory.*

Some may get concerned that we are downplaying the *Fall* and the gathering in of souls. Please do not go there and be at peace. We are not in any way downplaying or minimizing the importance and the role that the *Fall* and resulting *redemption* holds in our faith. The *fall* is one of the foundational stones of Christianity. We must never lose sight of our Lord's great sacrifice and HIS LOVE for us to be redeemed into the FATHER's Kingdom to overcome the Fall. And winning souls, bringing people back into the relationship that God had desired they have with Him in the beginning, is undoubtedly a significant reason and purpose for our existence in this world. But what we are saying is that as necessary as the *Fall* is, it is *one* stone in the foundation of God's *Ultimate Purpose and Plan* for us. It is not the whole *plan*. It is a critical and crucial part of THE plan for sure but still a part and not the whole.

As such, it is not a parking lot to park in, as so many Christians do, where they sit and wait for the Lord's return to carry them away to glory.

If man's central purpose is redemptive, then we are left with man—"redeemed," but *redeemed for what?* The answer must be "to get back onto the original path God intended for man to be on." Keep in mind. Our quest is not to question *redemption* but to find why God initially *created* us. Redemption is there, and it is real, but it is not the *Original Intention and Purpose* of God for creation.

With the *Fall* as the starting place, the result is a *man-to-God* relationship with God being dependent on man to sin so he can be redeemed. Under that starting point, our concern with God is, *"How does all this work for me?"* The modern philosophy seems to be that with redemption comes God's favor, and with God's favor comes having a "good" life. God has provided redemption to us, leading to a Christian life that is stress free, sacrifice free, and a happy lifestyle, a life that depends on what we see and get, in both this world and the next. It is an *all-about-me* story—which is, of itself, an unsatisfying, sordid story. This leaves everyone wondering, *Is that what Christianity is all about?* At that point, Christianity is no more than any other "social" redeeming idea.

A mindset develops that each of us has a *"God"* who exists just for and about our personal happiness and well-being. Therefore, when He does not make us happy, we believe that He has failed us. So in the back of our mind, we harbor the belief that God is not fair and, further, that God can fail, a slippery slope leading to a diminished definition of a God who is crippled by the failures of His own creation.

God has an Ultimate Purpose and Plan

Something inside us strongly believes that there is something more significant and better and of a grander nature in our relationship with God, our Creator. If man's purpose is to be redeemed, then that minimizes the meaning of creation and, ultimately, the purpose of God Himself. God is reduced to being a God who *made mistakes with His creation and therefore has to redeem His creation over and over.*

It is hard to believe that this is what God wants or created us for. Once we are redeemed, we want to "testify" and show others the joy of redemption—bringing them to the light of God and truth also. And that is a good thing; that is one thing we are instructed, as believers, to do, and every day of our life, we should be looking for those opportunities. But in addition to our "testimony," we must also be asking, "*What's next between You and me, God?*"

Because many do not ask this question, they receive no answer. Instead, they press into a pursuit of *meaningful service.* This produces a *sense* of purpose, a "Christian" career, a model for serving others. But again, where does the definition of *meaningful service* come from? From *man,* of course. It is what *man determines to be meaningful and what man determines to be service.* It remains a *man-to-God* relationship that tends to be self-gratifying, demoting God to a secondary, observer role.

Is that what God intended? To be an observer of His creation, sitting on the sideline, watching *man* struggle to fulfill his idea of *meaningful service?*

Again we ask that you do not get us wrong. *Meaningful service* is excellent and proper for believers to do, but *meaningful service* is not an end to itself but is a means to an end. What is that *end?* The real value of *meaningful service* to God is NOT in the service itself but in the attitude behind it that is driving one to do it.

In the Apostle Paul's letter to the believers at Ephesus, he wrote:

> *So be very careful how you live, not being like*
> *those with no understanding, but live honorably*
> *with true wisdom, for we are living in evil times.*

> *Take full advantage of every day as you spend your*
> *life for HIS PURPOSES.* (Ephesians 5:15–16 TPT)

We are told to *spend* our lives for *His purposes. Meaningful service,* therefore, is only *meaningful* if it fulfills God's purposes—not ours! To fulfill God's purposes, we need to know what *His purposes* are, and as we have seen, they are not found in either *creation* or the *fall.* We need to look deeper…further back…beyond the *fall*… beyond *creation.*

The "Great Before" as the Starting Place

So we must find a better *starting place.* But where is that? It must be before *creation.* If there is a story back beyond the creation, that story must begin in the *Great Before.*

> When was the *Great Before?*
>   We do not know.
> Where was the *Great Before?*
>   We do not know.
> What was the *Great Before?*
>   Ah, that one we know. It was the *shared glory of God.* Look at
>   what the *Diary* says:

> > *And now, O Father, glorify Me in Your own*
> > *presence with the glory which I had with You before*
> > *the world existed.* (John 17:5 NKJV)

This is the *SON* speaking! To the *FATHER!* Before *the world was*— before *creation*—this is the *Great Before.* Jesus and the Father shared in their *glory* together. It is a safe bet that knowing the Holy Spirit is the third member of the TRIUNE Godhead, HE was there also, and He shared in that *glory* along with the *SON* and the *FATHER.* Jesus is asking the FATHER to *restore* that *glory,* which means that the glory ended sometime after *"the world was."*

So we have a significant clue: *the Triune Godhead shared in glory during the Great Before creation, and it ended sometime after the world was created.*

Yes, a clue, but also it presents a problem, an apparent contradiction in purpose: if God wanted to create a universe for some positive reason, how is it creation worked to do the opposite and ended the *glory* They shared? It would not seem that God would plan that. How did that happen? What went wrong?

Is there something there in the *Great Before* that answers our question? How do we find and "get to" the *Great Before*?

We have the *Diary*. If there is an answer to be found to that question, the only place it will be is in the *Diary*. If so, the *Diary* will show us where the *starting place* is.

> *Making known to us the mystery of His will, according to His good pleasure, which He purposed in Himself, as a plan for the fullness of time, to unite all things in Christ, which are in heaven and on earth.* (Ephesians 1:9–10 MEV)

Time to hit the *Diary* again…

CHAPTER 4

THE "UNVEILING"

If we are going to uncover a *Purpose* for creation, we recognize the need to start with God rather than with man.

We have seen that starting at either *Creation* or the *Fall* does not answer our question and can quickly get us distracted away from our journey. We must get to the place where there is only God. That is where we will find the answers. What drove God to decide to *Create* when He did not have to? What was His *Ultimate Purpose*? We will only find that answer when there is God to answer.

And it is more than that. We tried creation where it "began" with God, but as soon as man got into the picture, he stole the show, and it became all about him. We need to get to the place where ONLY God existed, and it stayed as ONLY God. That must be *before* creation.

"In the beginning—God." Nothing else. Nothing less. It is not about man—it is all about God. If we are to understand God's original intent and purpose, we need to look at a platform that is about God and only God. God exists in the *Spiritual*. So long as we are on a *material* platform, we are on the wrong platform. In our search for the answer, we need to get off the *material* platform and get onto the *Spiritual* platform God is on—the platform God was on before the material platform came into existence.

Look at it from the perspective of an architect. If we wanted to know why an architect decided to build a particular structure at a specific site in a certain manner, we would not go and ask the builder.

Instead, we would ask the architect what drove him to make those decisions before giving the builder his building directions to build in that manner. Before a hammer strikes a nail, there is an idea. That idea births a plan. That plan results in the *creation* of the building. To understand God's concept regarding His *creation*, we must go back to before *a hammer strikes a nail.*

If the *Spiritual* platform is not found at the *Fall*, and if it is not found at *Creation*, where can that platform be found?

The bigger question is, how do we look? How do we find a *spiritual* platform when we are NOT *spirit* and are not even sure what it would look like?

To answer our question, we need to see into the *spiritual* realm. Is that possible? On our own, without some *divine* intervention, it is not. But remember, we have access to the *Creator's Diary,* and now that we know what to look for, maybe the *Creator* left some notes in the *Diary.*

The Spiritual Platform

It turns out, He did.

Searching the *Diary*, we find that the Apostle Paul answered that question two thousand years ago in his letter to the believers at the city of Ephesus:

> *Blessed be the God and Father of our Lord Jesus Christ, who has blessed us with every spiritual blessing in the heavenly places in Christ, just as He chose us in Him Before the foundation of the world, that we would be holy and blameless before Him. In love, He predestined us to adoption as sons through Jesus Christ to Himself, according to the kind intention of His will, to the praise of the glory of His grace, which He freely bestowed on us in the Beloved. And through the revelation of the Anointed One, he unveiled his secret desires to us—the hidden mystery of his long-range plan, which he was*

delighted to implement from the very beginning of time. (Ephesians 1:4–6, 9 TPT)

Whoa!! Hold everything! Did you hear what I just heard?

> *"Spiritual blessings...heavenly places" sounds like a spiritual platform to me. "Delighted to implement from the very beginning of time" sounds like the before too. "Revelation of the Anointed One, he unveiled his secret desires to us...hidden mystery of his long-range plan" sounds like His original intention and purpose. "Implement...from very beginning of time!"*

It sounds like the Holy Spirit allowed the Apostle Paul to listen in on a TRIUNE Godhead's private meeting about a *secret plan*—a *mystery* plan—that reveals the *architect's long-range* plans BEFORE He began building! It sounds like Paul was privileged to listen in on exactly what we are looking for—the answer to the big *Why.*

This Scripture gives a clear insight into the *intent* of God the Father—BEFORE creation. It is a peek, not only into God's mind but into the *secret* chambers of God's heart. We are clearly told that our history did not begin at *the Fall,* nor did it begin at *Creation* like we tend to think it did. Our history began BEFORE the *"foundations of the universe were even laid!"* BEFORE there was anything...BEFORE heaven...BEFORE earth, God made a *"long-range plan"* which HE was *"delighted to implement"* BEFORE He put anything into motion! And we are part of that plan!

We did not even exist, and HE had a *plan* for us to be *joined* with Him!

There it is—the Holy Spirit is giving us the *"unveiling of His secret desires"* concerning us! Before we were even *created!* That, ladies and gentlemen, is the *Architect's plan* before He gives it to the Builder. We are listening in on the Triune God telling us what was in His mind, what was His desire, what drove Him to create, long before He created the first blade of grass! Before *"a hammer struck a nail."*

So the plan was made, and all His creative activity would follow the plan. When we read in Genesis *"In the beginning—God,"* we
need to insert these verses from Ephesians. They are the BEFORE that
explains all that follows—His intent, His plan:

> *"In the beginning, God had his secret desires*
> *for us—the hidden mystery of his long-range plan,*
> *which he was delighted to implement from the very*
> *beginning of time when He said, 'Let there be.'"*

It is difficult for us to think BEFORE the foundations of creation.
Our carnal minds cannot wrap themselves around such an awesome
concept. We want to shout out in frustration, "How?" "When?"
"Where?" Man desires to know about God and what God is doing
and how that applies to him. But even though we do not understand
it, it resonates and we know there is truth in it and we place our faith
in God. Since we cannot understand the *hows, whats,* and *whens* of
His plan, we walk by faith because we see a *why*.

> *And without faith, it is impossible to please*
> *God, for he who comes to God must believe that He*
> *exists and that He is a rewarder of those who dili-*
> *gently seek Him.* (Hebrews 11:6 MEV)

We question how Paul knows such things about the *spiritual
platform* to speak about it so forcefully. But then we do not need to
wonder; he tells us in the *Diary*. In one of his letters, Paul wrote the
following:

> *Someone I'm acquainted with, who is in union*
> *with Christ, was swept away fourteen years ago in*
> *an ecstatic experience. He was taken into the third*
> *heaven, but I am not sure if he was in his body or*
> *out of his body—only God knows. And I know that*
> *this man (again, I'm not sure if he was still in his*
> *body or taken out of his body—God knows) was*

caught up in an ecstatic experience and brought into paradise, where he overheard many great and inexpressible secrets that were so sacred that no mortal is permitted to repeat them. I'm ready to boast of such an experience. (2 Corinthians 12:2–5 TPT)

"I am ready to boast of such an experience." That *"someone"* that Paul is *"acquainted"* with is none other than Paul himself. He is speaking of himself in the third person. This letter to the church at Corinth was one of the earliest letters in his ministry, likely written before AD 60. Paul clearly stated that the experience occurred "fourteen" years earlier. We know then that this "experience" would have occurred sometime in the mid-40s AD, only a decade following the death and resurrection of Jesus and shortly following Paul's encounter with Jesus on the road to Damascus.

Paul is now ready to *"boast"* about that experience. He is ready to tell us what happened—what he saw, what he heard, what he now knows and understands. And he does that not all at once. But from this time forward in each of his letters to the believers (*Ekklesia*) *"planted"* at Ephesus, Philippi, Colossi, and Rome, he gives a little bit. Paul speaks of *"mysteries"* that were revealed to him. Let us read that verse in Ephesians once again:

> *He unveiled his secret desires to us—the hidden mystery of his long-range plan, which he was delighted to implement from the very beginning of time.* (Ephesians 1:9 MEV)

And now look at what he wrote in his letter to the Colossians:

> *There is a divine mystery, a secret surprise that has been concealed from the world for generations, but now it's being revealed, unfolded, and manifested for every holy believer to experience.* (Colossians 1:27 MEV)

Paul was shown mysteries that had, up to this time, been hidden—"*concealed.*" One of those *mysteries* was the inclusion of the Gentiles—the whole world—into God's plan, and another one of those *mysteries* was the revealing of that plan—from "*the very beginning of time.*"

In his letters to the *Ekklesia* (churches), the Apostle Paul talks about the "*before.*" "*Before*" what? *Before the Fall, before creation, before the foundations, before* anything—when there was only God, only the Triune God and His boundless love. This is the *Great Before.*

> "*Eureka! We have found it! Here we find the
> answers we have been looking for!*"

The Hidden Mystery Unveiled

For us to know God's purpose in creation, we must not only begin at the beginning—at the *Great Before*—but we must get inside the heart of God and see from His viewpoint, not ours. His perspective is so radically different than our small, narrow view. He sees the whole picture, while we see only a piece. For centuries, man has only seen what was revealed directly in front of him as history marched by, and he has only caught glimpses of God's great plan. The Holy Spirit says, "*It was concealed from the world for generations, but now it's being revealed, unfolded and manifested.*" It is passing in front of us now, and we must see the whole picture to fully comprehend it.

Think of it this way: recall a day when you were in the middle of a crowded sidewalk, watching a parade passing by in front of you. From that vantage point, you see only that part of the parade passing directly in front of you. You see it for a time, and then it is gone. It comes, and it goes. You like (or dislike) what you see, what is in front of you at that moment. Then it moves on, and you see the next piece of the parade, and you get to like or dislike that moment of the parade. That is how we see our lives (and history), as a parade of events passing by in front of us. Some we enjoy, some we do not enjoy, but enjoy them or not, they pass on by as the next one takes its place in front of us. It can be difficult *connecting the dots* to understand the *theme (purpose)* of the parade (or our life).

Now let us take a different view. Climb aboard a helicopter and hover over the parade. Looking down, you see the whole parade unfolding below you. You can see the beginning of the parade, the middle of the parade, the end of the parade, and everything in between, and it all makes sense. You see the whole parade—all at the same moment. Amazing! You see the things you like and the things you do not like, and you have a real perception of what is going to be happening next that is better than now or that is worse than now. *You can connect the dots, and by doing so, you can understand the theme of the parade.*

That is the way God sees our lives.

Unfortunately, it is impossible for us to hover in a *helicopter* over our lives and see the beginning from the end, along with all the pieces in between. But through faith and the *Diary,* He is offering us to step into His *helicopter* and see creation from His viewpoint and interpret everything as it relates to His purpose and His plan. We open ourselves to understanding His plan as best as possible so that we recognize there is more to His plan beyond redemption. There is the whole *parade* as God planned it, and we get to watch and be a part of the fulfillment of all of that. *We see Creation, the Plan, the Fall, Redemption, Restoration, and the Resumption of the Plan.* We see the Beginning, and we see the End. And we see the Theme, the Purpose, of not only the parade but of our LIFE. What a Glorious ride God takes us on!

And we see *Father* smiling on His *children.* Life begins to take on a whole different look of what happens to us. When we learn to look from God's *helicopter* view, we begin to understand not only the what and the how of *creation* but the *why* of the Father's intention and His plan for implementation in the earth for His glory. As a result, we see less of *ourselves* and more of HIM.

For the first time, the focus is *God centered* and not *man centered.*

Paul's letter titled *Ephesians* is a *universal* letter, written to be circulated and read to all the *Ekklesia P*aul had planted. Reading it, we sense Paul's excitement at what he is revealing. The words jump off the pages in his enthusiasm! The majority of chapter 1 is actually one single sentence in the Greek, and Paul can only write a few words of that sentence at a time without breaking into praise and worship; he is so excited! In all his later Letters, Paul inserts truths and glimpses from his heavenly encounter, and he clearly shows us the purpose and intention of creation.

Just as He chose us in Him Before the foundation of the world, that we would be holy and blameless before Him. In love, He predestined us to adoption as sons through Jesus Christ to Himself, according to the kind intention of His will, to the praise of the glory of His grace, which He freely bestowed on us in the Beloved... And through the revelation of the Anointed One, he unveiled his secret desires to us—the hidden mystery of his long-range plan, which he was delighted to implement from the very beginning of time. (Ephesians 1:4–6, 9 NASB)

Giving thanks to the Father, who has enabled us to be partakers in the inheritance of the saints in light. He has delivered us from the power of darkness and has transferred us into the kingdom of His dear Son. (Colossians 1:12–13 NKJV)

Even the mystery which has been hidden from past ages and generations, but now is revealed to His saints. To them, God would make known what is the glorious riches of this mystery among the nations. (Colossians 1:26–27 MEV)

God, who has called you to His kingdom and glory. (1 Thessalonians 2:12 MEV)

We might become heirs according to the hope
of eternal life. (Titus 3:7 MEV)

Before the foundations of the world were laid,
God's Plan was for us (*who had not been created*
yet) to be *inheritors of His Kingdom!*

This is truly seeing into the heart of God—not only God the Creator, but God the Father—the *glory-sharing,* loving heart of FATHERLOVE.

Not His activities and manifestations, oh no! We are talking about the Person of God, the Father, the One and Only FATHERLOVE, the One who is first and foremost THE FATHER, having the original "*God to God*" relationship of FATHER-SON and desiring a "God to man" relationship of Father to sons.

God's Ultimate Purpose for Creation

From this starting place, looking out from the Father's heart, we see His eternal goal—to have adopted sons through Jesus, manifesting His glory!

God's original intention is to have a family!

Before anything existed, God intended to have "sons" "in Christ" to be joined with Him. Why? "*In love…the kind intention of His will.*" God desires to have "sons" in Christ, to be joined with Him, purely because of the love that He is and the "kindness" of His will to share His glory with you and me!

His ultimate intention is not only to *redeem* us but to have us "*co-inherit*" His *kingdom* along with His Beloved Son, *Yeshua HaMashiach—Jesus the Messiah.* This is far removed from a hierarchy relationship. It is a personal relationship, a relationship so close we are *joined* with Him as HIS *sons and daughters.*

Redemption is important—and necessary—to get us back unto the "*straight and narrow*" pathway that leads to the Kingdom. *Redemption* is not the endpoint; it is a *way station, a*n essential and necessary *way station* for sure. One needed to get us back into God's original plan of becoming part of His *family to share the glory of His LOVE.*

God's plan is a *Father-son* template, a template of a union between Him and His sons through His Begotten Son, Jesus.

All that the Father has in mind for His family of "sons" are *by, for*, and *through* His Beloved Son, *Yeshua*, who is the *centerpiece* of God's Kingdom. This is revealed in Paul's letter to the churches at Colossi about why God the Father made Jesus the *centerpiece* of all things. Jesus brought God to us and showed us God's way by His own life:

> *He is the image of the invisible God and the firstborn of every creature. For by Him all things were created that are in heaven and that are in earth, visible and invisible, whether they are thrones, or dominions, or principalities, or powers. All things were created by Him and for Him. He is before all things, and in Him all things hold together. He is the head of the body, the church. He is the beginning, the firstborn from the dead, so that in all things He may have the preeminence. For it pleased the Father that in Him all fullness should dwell, and to reconcile all things to Himself by Him, having made peace through the blood of His cross, by Him, I say—whether they are things in earth, or things in heaven.* (Colossians 1:15–20 MEV)

Take the time to read the Letter to the Colossians. It is short, and It radiates the Glory of Jesus!

God has chosen His Son, *Adonai Yeshua,* the Lord Jesus, to be His *centerpiece* in the universe. Everything God purposed is centered in His Son, done through the Son, for the Son, and unto the Son. God interprets everything about Himself and His purpose from the paternal Father's perspective of *Father-Son.*

It was the intention of God the Father that all men would find answers to all their life questions in Jesus Christ. Jesus Christ does not *have* the answers—HE IS THE ANSWER!

That is the joy of seeking Him and the fulfillment of knowing Him as our "*brother*," in addition to being our Savior and Lord.

Further revelation of God's plan with *Yeshua* as the *centerpiece* is revealed in Paul's Letter to the believers at Philippi.

In particular, note chapter 2, which is referred to as the Kenosis[2] passage, where Paul reveals *Yeshua* in all His godliness *before* He came to earth as man:

> *He existed in the form of God, yet he gave no thought to seizing equality with God as his supreme prize. Instead, he emptied himself of his outward glory by reducing himself to the form of a lowly servant. He became human! He humbled himself and became vulnerable, choosing to be revealed as a man and was obedient. He was a perfect example, even in his death—a criminal's death by crucifixion! Because of that obedience, God exalted him and multiplied his greatness! He has now been given the greatest of all names!* (Philippians 2:6–9 TPT)

He emptied Himself of all He was in heaven! He purposely laid all that aside and lived life like we live life to experience being overcomers in and through Jesus Christ. This is the PLAN as we advance in the Kingdom. To the Ephesians, the Apostle Paul said:

> *As a plan for the fullness of time, to unite all things in Christ, which are in heaven and on earth.* (Ephesians 1:10 MEV)

---

[2] In Christian theology, the renunciation of the divine nature, at least in part, by Christ in the Incarnation.

This was a follow-up to Jesus saying,

> *Your will be done in earth as it is in heaven.*
> (Matthew 6:10 MEV)

Since God's plans and purposes are not determined by man's needs but rather by God's desire for a *family* to share His *glory* and *love*, we see how all things in our lives take on new meaning when they are rightly related to Him, for Him, through Him, and unto Him—only.

Jesus was chosen by the Father to be the *centerpiece* of the universe for all men. The Father's purpose for the Son and the understanding of this *"mystery"* is a beautiful revelation:

- It overflows with the earlier *"glory"* that Jesus spoke about in John 17 and the Godhead shared *before the foundations of the world were laid.*
- It reveals what FATHERLOVE wants from His family of sons.
  - o   to be the Bride of His Beloved Son, *Jesus.*
- It reveals the corporate *"body of Christ"* and places *Yeshua* as the "head."
- And it reveals the plan of creation to expand the "glory" of the Father's Love.

God's ULTIMATE INTENTION *with Creation is…* FATHERHOOD.

God's ULTIMATE PURPOSE *with Creation is…coheir "sons" through Christ.*

God's ULTIMATE PLAN *with Creation is…Yeshua as the head of the family body.*

CHAPTER 5

IN HIS IMAGE

In the beginning, God created the heavens and the earth. The earth was without form and void, and darkness was on the face of the deep. And the Spirit of God was hovering over the face of the waters. Then God said, "Let there be light"; and there was light. (Genesis 1:1–5 NKJV)

And so begins our understanding of the creation process. The Hebrew word for *"in the beginning"* is *re'shivh,* and it means *the first* or *first fruit of creation.* God is the *first fruit* before creation itself. Before all creation, before all the foundations of the universe were laid, *He was, He is, and He always shall be...the Alpha and the Omega...the Beginning and the End...Always and Eternal!*

In ancient Hebrew thought and language, a name was more than a means of identification. It was a declaration of *what* a person was, their core personality—their character—their essence. God changed people's names as He changed them. Think of Abram and Sarai to Abraham and Sarah, and Jacob (*the schemer*) to Israel (*the people*).

In Scripture, God is referred to by many names, each one revealing another side of who and what He is. When Moses, kneeling in front of the burning bush, asked God, *"Who are you? Who do I tell the people sent me?"* God replied, "I Am. Tell them I Am sent you." This name is so sacred to the Hebrews that the consonants YHVH are used to express it in writing, and it is never spoken out loud. Among non-Jews, the name *Yahweh* has emerged as expressing it. It's meaning is all-encompassing and means *"He lives," "He always has, and He always will,"* or simply *"He is."*

To Moses, God is speaking in the first person, "I Am." The meaning is *"He who is self-existing—is."* In the ancient world, this concept of God was radical, and it is what separated "I Am" from the other gods of the world and, resultantly, the Hebrews from the rest of the world's population. Moses had asked for a name; he was given an expression of God's personality: *He who is self-existing—lives.*

In the first Book of the Holy Bible, Genesis—*which is named Re'shivh in the Torah (Hebrew Law Scriptures)*—God is called *Elohim.* Note that *Elohim* is the plural form. The name *Elohim* occurs over 2,600 times in the Tanakh[3] (Hebrew Bible). Being plural, God is presented as consisting of multiple dimensions. For Christians, Scripture delineates these dimensions as inclusive of three—the Father, the Son, and the Holy Spirit. Together, we refer to this as the Triune Godhead, or the Trinity. Whenever we see the word *Elohim* in reference to *YHVH*, it always has reference to the plural *Godhead.* Everything that is God is bundled into this name *Elohim*—the Trinity. He is three in one—separate and individual—yet united in the *Godhead.* It is the expression of who God was before the foundations of the universe were laid and who God is today. *Elohim is life, light, and love. And being life, He is the keeper of life, and only He can give life.*

"YHVH Elohim" is a common expression of God used in the Tanakh. It is interpreted as *"Lord God"* and carries the connotation of the All-Powerful, eternal, sovereign God who exists from the beginning.

A derivative title is also applied to God, which means *"to worship and adore."* *"Adonai Elohim"* is the only one to be worshiped and adored. God's followers are called to be worshippers of God. It is not so much what God does as it is *who* God is. And because of who God is, He is to be worshipped.

---

3   https://en.wikipedia.org/wiki/Hebrew_Bible.

This brief overview of God's name is important to us because shortly after *"In the beginning"* in the *Diary* comes

> *Then God said, "Let us make man and woman in our image, to be like us..." So, God created man and woman and shaped them with His image inside them. In His beautiful image, He created His masterpiece, Yes, male and female He created them.* (Genesis 1:26–27 TPT)

As stated in the opening of this chapter, names carry information as to character and identity. Being *created* in the image of God, by understanding His names, we identify our character.

In the previous chapters, we saw that *"before the foundations of the universe were laid,"* God had a plan of His intention that included us. In the first chapter of His *Diary*, we see Him putting His plan into action—*creation*. He creates the universe, the world, all the living flora, birds, and creatures that inhabit it. And God creates us. But He does so differently than all the previous creation. With the universe, the world, and the living creatures, He speaks the *Word*, and they came into existence. But not so with humans!

Oh, no, the creation of humans was personal with God.

> *Yahweh-God scooped up a lump of soil, sculpted a man, and blew into his nostrils the breath of life. The man came alive—a living soul.* (Genesis 2:7 TPT)

God *personally* forms man out of the dirt of the earth. Then God *personally* breathes life into his dirt body. God's breath is Spirit and Life—God breathed His Spirit-life into man, and man's physical dirt body came alive with the Spirit-life of God. Man is made in the *"image of God."* Nothing else in creation was created in God's image—only man.

And our soul cries out, *What is the image we are made into? What is God's image? Do I look like God? Do I think like God? Do I feel like*

God? What does it mean to be created in the image of God, and does that have any bearing on God's Purpose and Plan for me?

<u>What is the image of God?</u>

> *God is spirit, and those who worship him must worship in spirit and truth.* (John 4:24 MEV)

God is not physical; He is Spirit, so God's *image* cannot be physical or material.

And once again, we have a conflict, another apparent contradiction: man is not formed of Spirit but of the "*dust of the earth.*" So man is created *physical* from *material* in the "image of God." God is not physical or *material* but is a *spirit.* How are we then "*made in the image of God*"?

God formed man with a physical body made of material earth, then He "*breathed*" His Spirit-life into man's earthly body, and man became alive. By *breathing* His Spirit-life into man's material body, God made a way for His Spirit to reside *inside* of us. Is this instilled Spirit then being "*made in the image of God*"?

Searching the *Diary*, we find an interesting thing—this Spirit can be accepted or rejected by man on an individual basis:

> *Now we have not received the spirit of the world, but the Spirit who is from God, so that we may know the things that are freely given to us by God.* (Corinthians 2:12 MEV)

> *And because you are sons, God sent the Spirit of his Son into our hearts, who calls "Abba! Father!"* (Galatians 4:6 MEV)

> *By this, we know that we reside in God and he in us: in that he has given us of his Spirit.* (John 4:13 MEV)

But not everyone welcomes and follows the *Spirit* of God in them:

> For those who live according to the flesh have their outlook shaped by the things of the flesh, but those who live according to the Spirit have their outlook shaped by the things of the Spirit. (Romans 8:5 MEV)

> For all who are led by the Spirit of God are the sons of God. (Romans 8:14 MEV)

> The unbeliever does not receive the things of the Spirit of God, for they are foolishness to him. And he cannot understand them because they are spiritually discerned. (1 Corinthians 2:14 MEV)

> Consequently, the one who rejects this is not rejecting human authority but God, who gives his Spirit to you. (1 Thessalonians 4:8 NASB)

God has *"breathed"* a touch of *His Spirit* into us, which we then have the *free will* to accept and even increase by allowing the Holy Spirit to enter our spirits. This is what God desires for us to do as He moves us along the path to becoming more like Christ which, if you recall, is part of His *Ultimate Purpose* and *Plan*. Unfortunately, we also have the *free will* to reject His Spirit, which moves us along the path of becoming less like Christ, creating cold, hard, unloving hearts becoming more self-centered, and the *Spirit* of God within us *decreases.*

Part of our creation is physical, but that *physical* is not the image of God since God is a spirit. What we physically look like is what God wanted *man* to look like, thousands of years into the future, when God would send His Son into the world as a human.

Conversely, we are given a *touch* of God's Spirit that gives us life and ignites a spirit within us. But we do not exist in this world as a spirit, and while providing life to the physical body, this Spirit can be accepted or rejected on an individual basis. It would appear that being *created* in *"the image of God"* is neither physical, nor spiritual.

Made in the Image of God

If it is not physical and not totally spiritual, what is the *"image of God"*? We need to broaden our definition of the word *image* from *visible, physical appearance* to *shadowing or emulating other characteristics.* Both are accepted meanings of the word *image.*

Being made in the *image* of God is how we were created. God is the Triune Godhead—Father, Son, and Holy Spirit. Man was created as a *triune being* also, consisting of body, spirit, and soul. God made us in His *image* by imparting some of His Spirit along with some of His characteristics and personality into our creation. It consists of characteristics that make man different from the rest of creation.

We submit that this is one of the most beautiful, glorious truths and concepts in the entire Holy Scriptures, that God *created* us to possess key characteristics HE possesses!

What are these characteristics? The *Diary* tells us clearly what His attributes are. The Holy Spirit inspired men to write about God using a mantra of names, each of which showcased God's various characteristics, telling us who He is.

Many of these attributes are not transferable to people, belonging to God alone, for example:

- *Elohim*—the divine Triune Godhead of Creation,
- *El Shaddai*—the Almighty God,
- *El Olam*—the Eternal God,
- *El Elyon*—God Most High,
- *Adonai*—the Lord Master,
- *Yahweh Shalom*—the God of Peace,
- *Yahweh Yireh*—the God Provider,
- *Yahweh Rophe*—the God Healer,
- *Yahweh Tsebaoth*—the God of Hosts,
- *Yahweh Roi*—the God my Shepherd,

- *Yahweh Tsuri*—the God my Rock,
- *Yahweh Nissi*—God my Banner,
- *Yahweh Tsidqenu*—the God of Righteousness, and
- *El Kanna*—God the consuming Fire.

Those attributes, and others, are incommunicable and define Him alone. They are what make God, GOD, and they are not transferable to *man*. Under no circumstances should anyone think we are made to be "gods"—we are not. God is the All-knowing, All-powerful, Omnipotent, Sovereign Creator, and we are His creation, plain and simple.

But there are other attributes of God that are communicable, that He can and does share with His created man, characteristics that mold us into the loving nature of God and separate us from the rest of creation, characteristics that give us the *image* of God.

For example, we know that God can think, reason, and make decisions. So man also was made in the *image* of God with the ability to think, reason, and make decisions. It is true; no one knows the mind of God. His thoughts are far removed from, far above ours, but what He gave us is remarkable on its own. The sense of wondering about the universe around us and seeking answers and having the mental ability and freedom to accept or reject things (even rejecting the Creator Himself) are things no other living creature possesses. When is the last time you saw a gorilla design a car? Or a cow staring at the night sky to pick out the constellations?

God gave man *"dominion"* over the world and told man to *"subdue"* it. God's *image in man* is reflected in our ability to *govern creation with power, wisdom, and understanding, all attributes of God.* Over the centuries of recorded history, man has harnessed the wonders and wealth of the world. Iron, steel, energy, medicine, biology, agriculture, and all the sciences have grown to reveal the marvels and wonders of creation. Man has *"subdued"* the world by harvesting the bounty of known and unknown, seen and unseen wonders and treasures God made in creation. Man has ventured forth into space to explore the vastness of creation beyond the physical boundaries and limits of earth.

Unfortunately, man has not always been a "good" caretaker of these resources and discoveries and has developed them at a high cost to creation itself so that all *"creation groans"* under man's many times poor oversight and *"dominion."*

We seek the beauty and artistry God showed in creating all things and created in His image; we seek to recreate such beauty ourselves through the arts, music, science, and technology.

God created man and woman and put His image of LOVE inside of them. God is love. Love is His image. He created Adam and then Eve as His masterpieces. Love is inside of man and woman. Love and unity together. Together they are one! The natural world moves and responds to rigid *instincts*, such as migrating ten thousand miles without knowing why. But man and woman respond to LOVE, kindness, and heartfelt caring for one another. The first expression of who Adam and Eve are is unity—love. They are "ONE"—together—no longer "one and one are two" but "ONE AND ONE" ARE ONE.

In the TRIUNE GODHEAD, $1 + 1 + 1 = 1$. That is the image of God. And that is what Jesus prayed to the FATHER in John 17—that we also be as one with them.

The word *Adam* means *humanity*. Adam is humanity's father—Adam…man…mankind. Adam is made in the Father's image of LOVE. Adam and Eve together are Adam. They are not separate—they are one. Adam is made to make. *"In his image"* means he is a *reflection* of the LOVE of He who made him. Humanity reflects FATHERLOVE.

Adam and Eve become the reflection of God's creative power. When God planted the garden, everything was fully grown, and from that, HE could lay out the principle of seed-bearing. All the trees bore seed, and the seed that was born grew more of the same kind. Oak trees developed oak trees. Palm trees produced palm trees. Whatever it is, when God planted it in its full-grown process, it held the seed to make more of its own kind. That is the principle in creating Adam and Eve. Their planted seed grew humanity—after their image, which is after God's image.

The Son is the dazzling radiance of God's splendor, the exact expression of God's true nature—

his mirror image! He holds the universe together and expands it by the mighty power of his spoken word. (Hebrews 1:3 TPT)

As *"sons and daughters"* of a holy and righteous Creator, we carry a responsibility to reflect the *"image"* of the Creator on earth:

> *As a prisoner of the Lord, I plead with you to walk holy, in a way that is suitable to your high rank, given to you in your divine calling. With tender humility and quiet patience, always demonstrate gentleness and generous love toward one another, especially toward those who may try your patience. Be faithful to guard the sweet harmony of the Holy Spirit among you in the bonds of peace, being one body and one spirit, as you were all called into the same glorious hope of divine destiny. For the Lord God is one, so are we, for we share in one faith, one baptism, and one Father. And He is the perfect Father who leads us all, works through us all, and lives in us all.* (Ephesians 4:1–6 TPT)

One of the most generous gifts the Creator bestowed on humankind, reflecting His *image* is the freedom to make decisions of choice. Of all the thousands of living creatures of creation, only man was created as a *free moral agent.* We are endowed with a sense of *right and wrong* and of *good and evil.* We can nurture that sense in either direction. We do not just exist and react to instinct as the animal kingdom does, but we think and ponder. Our soul *seeks* to know its Creator and yearns to understand our role in all of creation.

Along with this *gift* comes the dark ability to reject good and embrace evil by allowing *fleshly* desires to grow, foster, and take root in our souls if we allow them to. God's passion is for us to seek after Him and His righteousness, but in His magnificence, grace, and love, He allows us to choose. How it must break His heart to see us turn away and seek after the temporal, carnal things of this world.

Created in the *"Image of God"* is intended to bring the same Godly attributes exhibited in heaven to earth. Such is the *"Kingdom of God on earth as in heaven."* *Yeshua HaMashiach—Jesus the Messiah—* ushered in the Kingdom two thousand years ago.

It is part of God's *Original Intention* that we promote the *Kingdom* into the world as His *inherited sons*. Being created in God's image laid the foundation, the groundwork, and set the stage for God's *Ultimate Purpose* and *Plan* to be implemented.

CHAPTER 6

CAUGHT, NOT TAUGHT

"If our words do not match our actions, then our audience cannot hear what we are saying because our actions are drowning out our words."[4]

Before we move forward with the revelation of the *"hidden mystery"* as unveiled to the Apostle Paul, we would like to briefly discuss the concept of *Caught, not Taught,* as it becomes of significant importance in our revelation of God's *Ultimate Intention, Purpose, and Plan.*

In chapter 1 of the Book of Acts, the Apostle Luke opened his writings to Theophilus, stating that he was recording *"all the things that Jesus did and taught."* Notice he said *"did"* before he said *"taught."* While on the surface, that may seem insignificant, it is a particularly important sequence.

Today, we would almost certainly say the reverse—what Jesus *taught and did.* In our world, almost without exception, the *teaching* comes first, and then the *doing.*

The significance of what Doctor Luke is telling us is, the things that Jesus did were His teachings. In other words, Jesus taught by doing. Even better said is, Jesus taught by BEING. He did not *teach* them to LOVE—He is LOVE. They saw His LOVE for the people—for

---

4   Source of quote is unknown.

the sick, the depressed, the oppressed—and they *Caught* His love for them.

He did not explain feeding ten thousand people with five small fish and two loaves of bread. No, He blessed the offering and gave it to the disciples to distribute, and *it* happened! *It* happened because of His compassion for the people who had not eaten and not because heaven had some baskets of fish and bread hanging around. The disciples *Caught* that lesson, not the *lesson* of multiplication but the *lesson* of hunger.

He did not teach them how to cast out demons, showing the necessary steps from the *how to cast out demons, 101 Primer*. He did it, and they learned. They learned the *compassion* for those who were possessed, and they learned the *freedom* of those set free.

The things Jesus did and the actions He took were the *basis* of His *teaching* to the disciples. How He lived; how He fed them, treated them, and worked with and around them; how He dealt with the people, the diseases, the demons, and the religious authorities *caused the disciples to learn those powerful unspoken messages of compassion, character, values, and LOVE.* Any questions they may have had would result in a parable for the explanation.

He told them not to do as the Pharisees did, who said one thing and did another. He gave them the principles and values of life by the example of His life. *Those principles were then written on the tablets of their (and our) hearts:*

> *Do not let mercy and truth forsake you; bind them around your neck, write them on the tablet of your heart so that you will find favor and good understanding in the sight of God and man.* (Proverbs 3:3–4 NKJV)

> *Your word I have treasured in my heart, That I may not sin against You.* (Psalm 119:11 MEV)

Certain things do not lend themselves easily to being *taught.* They can only be "*written on our hearts*" by being *caught.* These things tend to be the motivators behind actions. The *values* and *character-istics* result in situations—like hunger resulting in a miracle feeding of thousands. The disciples learned these values and characteristics as being *Caught, not Taught*.

The question is, how did He teach those things that became *Caught* as *Taught*? And the answer is, there is a *secret* to the "*Caught, not Taught*" concept and principle. A *secret* so powerful that without it, it does not work.

The "*Caught, not Taught*" Secret

What is that *secret*?

The *secret* is, "*Who is playing catch with whom?*"

The game of *catch* is initiated by the Holy Spirit. The Holy Spirit is the "pitcher."

And He is *pitching* to the human *spirit*. The human spirit is the "catcher."

God bypasses the human mind. It is "Spirit to spirit" communi-cation that is alive and vibrant. It is supernatural, devoid of thinking, logic, and rationale. It stands on *faith, belief,* and that *inner* knowl-edge of being made in the *image* of God, and with that *image* comes the revelation and power of "catching" things beyond human under-standing that mostly cannot be put into words.

Allow the human *mind* to get involved, and the game comes to a sudden halt. When Peter stepped out of the boat, he allowed the *Holy Spirit* to *pitch* directly to his *spirit,* and he walked on water. When he saw the waves, he allowed his mind to get into the "game," and he sunk.

It is like playing that childhood game *pickle in the middle,* with the human mind being the *pickle* trying desperately to get into the *game.* Do not let *him* in. Keep the ball moving from the Holy Spirit of God to the God-breathed spirit inside of you. You do not need your mind for this game. It will only cause you to sink.

To catch anything, the one doing the *catching* must be aware that something is being thrown to them, and they must be prepared to receive it. This implies that there is someone on the other end communicating that something is going to be sent. That someone on the *pitching* end is the Holy Spirit—God. That someone on the *catching* end is the spirit God breathed into you. Therefore, we must always keep our spirit in contact with the Holy Spirit. This is done by prayer, the WORD, and an ongoing 24/7 relationship between Spirit and spirit.

For the things of GOD and the things of the KINGDOM, "Caught, not Taught" is not only the primary *teaching* method, it is the ONLY teaching method. They are Holy Spirit teachings. They are the *things* that words cannot do justice to, the things that settle in the heart and not the mind—the *things* of LIFE and LOVE. We do not want to say *feelings* because they go way beyond *feelings*, but when they are *caught*, there is a *feeling* that comes with them, a *feeling* unlike any other, one that draws our attention and lets us know that something unusual is happening. It is a *wake-up* call telling us to get prepared; a "pitch" is about to come. They create a whole new set of values that superimpose over all the earthly values our soul has learned, and we *feel* that we *grow* from that. We *learn* something in our hearts that our minds cannot process. That *something* is another level of agape LOVE.

Things *caught* are no longer mere *information* but are truths of WHO and WHAT God is. They are the foundational and fundamental building blocks of our "walk" with Christ going forward. Every time we *catch* a new truth, we grow in becoming more like Him, of being more of *who* HE is and filled with the revelation, knowledge, and power of the Holy Spirit.

"Caught, not Taught" is the most potent maturing process we can have in our life. It is steeped in the principles of the Kingdom of God and not of this world. It *teaches* by planting seeds in our hearts, seeds that grow into blossoms of LOVE for our fellow man, and that LOVE then results in the faith, the resolve, and the power to produce phenomenal results.

Everything Jesus did, He did at the *will* and *bequest* of the FATHER. And that pleased the FATHER, so much so that on three separate occasions, God audibly spoke His pleasure with Jesus (*Luke 3:23, Matthew 17:5, John 12:28*). How did that happen? The Holy Spirit "settled" on Jesus when He came up out of the water, and nothing Jesus did from that time on was done without the Holy Spirit.

This revealed the pattern of Father-Son teaching utilizing the "Caught, not Taught" concept. In turn, this is a natural outshoot of the principle "like Father, like Son." Jesus expanded the pattern of Like Father—Like Son to "Like Father—Like Son—Like disciple."

The template developed under this principle is that God's ways, the Words of God, and a Godly lifestyle are not only better Caught than Taught but are not taught any other way.

The principle of the Father is a living demonstration of the principle of "Caught, not Taught." Jesus and God are "*like Father, like Son.*" Jesus *catches* what the FATHER *pitches.* The FATHER is LOVE; Jesus *catches* that LOVE, and together with the Holy Spirit, they change people. *Changing* people results from being Caught, not Taught.

Teachings do not change people; "Catchings" do.

We characterize ourselves as being *"created in God's image."* Accepting Christ as Savior, Lord, and Master places us into the God family. As children in the *family,* we encounter the *lessons* of our Lord, and maturity comes by us *catching* them from the Holy Spirit when He throws them at us. Therefore, we must always be ready, willing, and able to *catch.* If we are not, then we miss out.

This should give us pause to reflect that what we do is more important than what we say as experience has proven that actions that are taught by words catch more. This pandemic of COVID-19 is a perfect example as so many of our *leaders* have issued orders and directives regarding not traveling, going out to eat, gathering in meetings, etc. They then turn around and violate their own directives. As a result, the *wrong lesson* is *caught* and people violate the orders and the pandemic spreads. And the leaders scratch their heads, not understanding why.

There is the "God family to the human family," and there is the "earthly father family to sons' family." God desires to have a family of "sons" who can and will co-inherit with Christ the kingdom. For this to happen, we need the Holy Spirit to be engaged with our spirit constantly. Only by that can we become more in the "image of Christ."

Thereby comes the title of this book: *Created by Love—Created to Love, Like Father—Like Sons*

The problem with today's world is there are too few "pitchers" in the families. Fathers are missing, Mothers are working, and most *teaching* is "do as I say, not do as I do."

Unfortunately, the *lessons* are well learned.

They *Catch* that the family *chooses* to be overly busy so that they cannot spend time with a grandparent each week. If we merely talk about the values we have without enacting them, there is no learning, and in fact, there are no values.

The principle of "*taught, not caught*"

If we begin with being *taught* and miss the *caught* part, we may get a lot of useful knowledge. We learn many Bible stories and history, psalms and songs of praise and worship, good life-living advice, and soundbites. It may even be learning about Jesus and the incredible knowledge about who almighty God is through Jesus Christ.

All that will be the best kind of thinking and knowledge that you will ever gain in all your life, BUT if it does not change your thinking, it will not change your life, and if it does not change your life, then it is of no value. It will serve you nothing. It will not *transform* you from an *earthly*, carnal person into a "*child of the Most High God Almighty*."

As we continue our journey to uncover the "*mystery*" hidden for ages, we will see how the concept of "*Caught, not Taught*" applies to the *Ultimate Intention, Purpose, and Plan* of God for creation on both the individual level and the corporate body of believers.

And we will see how Holy Spirit is "*Caught, not Taught*" as a life-changing, transformational experience that moves us toward becoming "*more like Jesus.*"

CHAPTER 7

FATHERLOVE

Within the pages of this book, we have taken the liberty to use a phrase in our presentation of God that is not familiar to you. That phrase is FATHERLOVE, and you are due an explanation of what that means to us. We will attempt to do that here, although words fall far short of expressing the depth and intensity of what we mean when we use the phrase.

First, let us be clear that it is NOT a title or a name. We have not renamed God as *"Father Love"* like some eastern guru or some mystical cult leader. No such disrespect or implication is intended or implied.

"FATHERLOVE" is our expression of GOD.

<u>What God is</u>

Above all things, the single most obvious principle in creation is that "GOD IS LOVE."

> *Those who are loved by God, let his love continually pour from you to one another because God is love. Everyone who loves is fathered by God and experiences an intimate knowledge of him. The one who doesn't love has yet to know God, for God is love. The light of God's love shined within us when*

he sent his matchless Son into the world so that we might live through him. This is love: He loved us long before we loved him. It was his love, not ours. He proved it by sending his Son to be the pleasing sacrificial offering to take away our sins." (1 John 4:7–10 TPT)

God does not *possess* love—GOD IS LOVE. From start to finish, from Alpha to Omega, from existence to creation, everything God does…thinks…acts upon…and gives is…LOVE. He exists for LOVE, HE plans for LOVE, and His *purpose* is LOVE. All God desires to do is to SHARE THIS overflowing fountain of LOVE. HE shares it with HIS SON, and they call it their *"glory."* HE shares it with the Holy Spirit, and they call it the *"fruit"* of the Spirit. HE shares it in heaven with all the angels and heavenly hosts. HE shares it by and with *creation*, and HE desires to share it throughout all the universe for all of eternity—with ALL who will be willing to *share* with HIM.

The second most apparent principle in creation is that GOD is the *Ultimate FATHER.*

He is the "first-fruit" of ALL things—spiritual and material. HE is the "seed" maker and giver. All creation, both in the heavens and the earth, originate in HIM. All *seeds* planted come from HIM—*seeds* of the universe (seeds of galaxies, solar systems, planets, and stars), *seeds* of earth life (of trees and forests, glens, and meadows), *seeds* of every species of animal life (birds in the sky, fish in the oceans, and all the teaming life, seen and unseen, on, in, and over the earth). Everything HE created is beautiful, majestic, breathtaking, and wonderful. The intricacies and complexities of created life together form a symphony of LOVE for and of LIFE, and He is *Seed* to all.

HE is SEED to all the human races—Brown, Black, White, Red, Yellow, tall, short, fat, thin, happy, sad, introspective, or extroverted. HE is FATHER to all, each and every one.

And HE LOVES every person—from the beginning of time to the last person who will be birthed on earth—just as much as HE LOVES HIS Begotten SON! Allow your mind to wrap around that thought for a minute and think of the magnitude of the "fountain" of LOVE that flows out from the FATHER!

HE IS both the *perfect* FATHER...and the PERFECTION of LOVE. HE IS "FATHERLOVE." It is not a title; it is WHO and WHAT HE IS.

In the *Diary*, there are three words used to express what in English we call *love*. There is *eros*, which is a *fleshly, carnal love* we are familiar with. There is *phileo*, which is a *"brotherly, kindly, caring love for one another."* And there is *agape*, which is an *"all-encompassing sacrificial love that surpasses and exceeds human capability."*

Agape is *supernatural* love, so powerful and so overwhelming few humans understand it—fewer still have experienced it. When used in Scripture, it almost always refers to a LOVE attribute of God.

> *For this is how much God loved (agape) the world—he gave his one and only, unique Son as a gift. So now everyone who believes in him will never perish but experience everlasting life.* (John 3:16 TPT)

Think about the LOVE expressed in that single statement!

Before the *"foundations of the world"* were laid, the Triune God—the *Creator* of ALL things!—shared Their *love* and *glory* among Themselves. God wanted to *create man, in His own image,* to allow man, *without being forced,* to share in that love and glory, even though He knew by doing so, it would bring Him heartache and pain. God further opened Himself up to be disappointed and hurt by giving His creation the free, unconstrained gift of "free will choice" to those He created in *"His own image"* and then giving them options to choose from—options that HE knew would bring deep pain and sorrow to HIMSELF. HE did not have to do this. Was not forced to do this. He did so, all on His own, and all because HE only wanted to share HIS LOVE—*voluntarily.*

That is FATHERLOVE.

God *loved* His creation of man and woman so much that He gave them the most incredible gift of all—*the ability and freedom to choose,* even if it meant rejecting Him as their Creator and God. And then, in a genuine agape love gesture, He gave options to choose from: two *trees* in the garden—one tree to follow Him, and the other tree to follow *self.*

They chose *self.*

But God's love exceeded their choice—and HE gave HIS SON as atonement for their poor choice.

And it was not finished. Before the *foundations of the universe were laid*—before there was *anything,* except God—He knew that HE would give us choices to choose from too, and that we would also make the wrong choices. He knew that He would have to sacrifice His only begotten Son to redeem us—His created "*sons and daughters*" who would use the *gift He freely gave* to us to turn our backs on Him. And yet He went ahead and did it anyway! God was solely in control, meaning He could have changed the template at any time—even before He started it—but He did not…because He loved us so. Such love, the world has never known! This is the essence of FATHERLOVE.

The *Father's* image is an image of love, so man was created in the *image* of the Father's love. He did all this before He created a single atom.

As mentioned earlier, *Elohim* is plural and consists of the Godhead—the Trinity—a relationship. The first characteristic we learn about God is that He IS a relationship. *"In the beginning, Elohim."* Who is *Elohim? Elohim* is Father, Son, and Holy Spirit.

How does God's characteristic of relationship fit into being created in His *image?*

God's original "template" was to *share* and *expand* the Triune Godhead's glory and love. Above all things, God is Father. That aspect of being *Father* caused Him to breathe life into man when He created him. Man wants a *Father.* He yearns for the FATHER. And further, man wants to be a *father.*

In addition to "having" God's *image* of love, reasoning, and free will "planted" inside of us, being *created* in the *image of God* is being created in the full *image of Father*, and therefore *fatherhood* is ingrained in us as the basis of *family* relationship.

The Hebrew word for *father* is *ab*, and it is used over 630 times in the Tanakh (Hebrew Bible). *Father* is the first word in the Hebrew language. But of all those uses in the Old Testament, only a small handful refers to God as *Father*, and then only in an overly broad, general manner. *Elohim* was the *Father* of creation…of the universe… of a nation.

Father is God's name. In 1 and 2 Peter, He is called *"God the Father"* and *"Father God."* Every mention of God in Scriptures is an expression of all that God is—the Father, the Son, and the Holy Spirit. Every mention of Him as *God* is a reference to the Godhead. So when you read *God*, it includes the Holy Spirit's ministry, the rulership of the Son, and established in the authority of Almighty God. Jesus said: *"If you have seen Me, you have seen the Father."* And He further said HE only says what the Father says and only does what the Father does.

Moses, when speaking to rebellious Israel, said,

> *Is not He your Father who has bought you? He has made you and established you. Remember the days of old. Consider the years of all generations. Ask your father, and he will inform you, your elders, and they will tell you.* (Deuteronomy 32:6–7 NASB)

So everything about God is about our *Father*, and he recognizes us as His children. And the Son is the favorite of the Father, which is also part of the Fatherhood principle.

David, the warrior psalmist, a *"man after God's own heart,"* wrote,

> *You are the righteous God who helps us like a father. Everyone everywhere looks to you, for you are the confidence of all the earth, even to the farthest islands of the sea.* (Psalm 65:5 TPT)

Our faithful and loving God waited for Israel to cry out for the Father's help:

> *Yet, even so, you waited and waited, watching to see if they would turn and cry out to you for a father's help. And then, when you heard their cry, you relented, and you remembered your covenant, and you turned your heart toward them again, according to your abundant, overflowing, and limitless love.* (Psalm 106:44–45 TPT)

The Israelites did not know God as a personal *Father*. They knew Him as *YHVH*—the great "*I AM*" who was to be feared and not spoken to and of whom one did not even say His name! In the wilderness, God told Moses that HE would "*show Himself*" and "*speak*" to the people. But when HE did, the people ran in fear and told Moses, "*We do not want to hear from God, you speak to Him for us.*" And so it was, and so it has been for many centuries. Man did not talk to God directly—*as a son to father*—but through intercessors, priests, and prophets. *But that was never God's plan or intention.* God wanted a one-on-one relationship with His sons and daughters.

The FATHER Relationship

So God sent His Son to the earth—as a man—and Jesus *turned the world upside down* by speaking of God as *His Father*, and as their *Father*, and as *THE FATHER* and as *our Father*. He did it so much that in three short years of ministry, it is recorded hundreds of times!

For Jesus, *Father* was personal.

> *Now the Word became flesh and took up residence among us. We saw his glory—the glory of the one and only, full of grace and truth, who came from the Father.* (John 1:14 NKJV)

I am the true vine, and my Father is the gardener. (John 15:1 NIV)

I testify about myself, and the Father who sent me testifies about me. (John 8:18 NIV)

Jesus replied, "If I glorify myself, my glory is worthless. The one who glorifies me is my Father, about whom you people say, 'He is our God.'" (John 8:54 NIV)

Righteous Father, even if the world does not know you, I know you, and these men know that you sent me. (John 17:25 NIV)

All things have been handed over to me by my Father. No one knows the Son except the Father, and no one knows the Father except the Son and anyone to whom the Son decides to reveal him. (Matthew 11:27 NKJV)

Jesus said to her, "Do not cling to Me, for I have not yet ascended to My Father; but go to My brethren and say to them, 'I am ascending to My Father and your Father, and to My God and your God.'" (John 20:17 NKJV)

Through accepting God's Son as Savior, Lord, Master, and Messiah, man is given the gift of a loving relationship with God—the FATHER:

For God so loved the world, that He gave His only begotten Son, that whoever believes in Him shall not perish, but have eternal life. (John 3:16 NKJV)

Jesus replied, "I am the way, and the truth, and the life. No one comes to the Father except through me." (John 14:6 NKJV)

For whoever does the will of my Father in heaven is my brother and sister and mother. (Matthew 12:50 NKJV)

Everyone who believes that Jesus is the Christ has been fathered by God, and everyone who loves the father loves the child fathered by him. (1 John 5:1 NKJV)

Yet for us, there is one God, the Father, from whom are all things and for whom we live, and one Lord, Jesus Christ, through whom are all things and through whom we live. (1 Corinthians 8:6 TPT)

See what sort of love the Father has given to us: that we should be called God's children—and indeed we are! For this reason, the world does not know us: because it did not know him. (1 John 3:1 NASB)

I have written to you, children, that you have known the Father. I have written to you, fathers, that you have known him who has been from the beginning. (1 John 2:14 NIV)

The Spirit himself bears witness to our spirit that we are God's children. (Romans 8:16 NKJV)

These Scriptures call attention to the essential message of the Fatherhood of God and establishes the pattern of Father-Son, which creates the principle of "like Father, like Son."

So, I kneel humbly in awe before the Father of our Lord Jesus, the Messiah, the perfect Father of

every father and child in heaven and on the earth.
(Ephesians 3:14 TPT)

The principle of the church family, (the *Ekklesia*), is to follow the principle of "Father—like Son": There is God, the Father; Father to the church. Then there is Jesus—Bride to the church family. Then there is the church family; *father* to the *human family*. God's Plan is complete: Father—like family. It only lacks human acceptance.

> *And now He alone is the leader and source of everything needed in the church. God has put everything beneath the authority of Jesus Christ and has given Him the highest rank above all others. And now we, His church, are His body on the earth, and that which fills Him, who is being filled by it!*
> (Ephesians 1:22–23 TPT)

The Father is the one who leads us. That is a "*Kingdom* realm" principle demonstrated in earth as it is in heaven. The Godhead sees themselves the same in both realms—the Spirit and the earthly realm. Look closely at the prayer Jesus gave His disciples:

> *Our Father who is in heaven, hallowed be Your name.*
> *Your kingdom come; Your will be done on earth, as it is in heaven.*
> *Give us this day our daily bread. And forgive us our debts, as we forgive our debtors.*
> *And lead us not into temptation but deliver us from evil.*
> *For Yours is the kingdom and the power and the glory forever. Amen.* (Matthew 6:10–13 NKJV)

Jesus is clearly showing us that The FATHER's Kingdom reigns in both realms—heaven and earth—and that we, His children, can live a life full of Him in both realms. How exciting is that!?

The Apostle Paul started his letter to the Ephesians with "*father*":

> *Paul, an apostle of Jesus Christ by the will of God, To the saints who are in Ephesus, and faithful in Christ Jesus: Grace to you and peace from God our Father and the Lord Jesus Christ. (Ephesians 1:1 NKJV)*

By doing so, Paul was revealing God's *sharing* of Himself, taking the position of fatherhood. It was not God's wonderful attributes or activities that Paul began with; it was God's Personage as *Father*, the unchanged Personage of LOVE—FATHERLOVE.

In the *Diary*, the Apostle Peter talked about celebrating the Father of our Lord Jesus Christ:

> *Blessed be the God and Father of our Lord Jesus Christ, who according to His great mercy has caused us to be born again to a living hope through the resurrection of Jesus Christ from the dead, to obtain an inheritance which is imperishable and undefiled and will not fade away, reserved in heaven for you, who are protected by the power of God through faith for a salvation ready to be revealed in the last time.* (1 Peter 1:3–5)

HE is first and foremost the FATHER, and everything that flows from the seed, flows from the FATHER. The FATHER seed is planted on the earth by men to create a son like the FATHER had a Son. And the Apostle Paul continued in his letter to the Ephesians:

> *So, I kneel humbly in awe before the Father of our Lord Jesus, the Messiah, the perfect Father of every father and child in heaven and on the earth.*

And I pray that He would unveil within you the unlimited riches of His glory and favor until supernatural strength floods your innermost being with His divine might and explosive power. (Ephesians 3:14–16 TPT)

Paul recognized that Father is foremost all that is God.

When we begin to read the Scriptures from the Father's paternal viewpoint and to recognize the Father's purpose and intention, then we begin to have an eternal view of man with a goal of Father-son. Everything takes on full meaning when we see the paternal view of the eternal Father. A man has a father. A son has a father; the son becomes a father. The ultimate intention is for all men to be fathers. A family of fathers and sons (children), growing together, comprising the body of Christ. FATHERLOVE to both Bride and Groom. 1 + 1 + 1 = 1; United in LOVE.

God is love, not loving…but LOVE. LOVE is not a description of God; it is the essence of *what* and *who* God is. *Agape LOVE is the unselfish, total, sacrificial giving of oneself for the greatest good to another.* It is not a sentimental or romantic expression of love but a conscious CHOICE to be forever *other-centered.*

Agape LOVE is all the FATHER knows.

God's desire to share is like the highest-purity diamond, cut and polished to replicate and reflect His *"unapproachable"* light (love) throughout all of creation, not for self-admiration or exaltation but for freely giving and expanding the pure, unselfish *glory* and *joy* that the sharing of such Love brings to the FATHER.

That is FATHERLOVE.

And God's *Purpose* and *Plan* for us—His "sons and daughters"—is for us to be high-purity diamonds, cut and polished by the Holy Spirit to reflect His dazzling, sparkling LOVE throughout all of creation.

That too is FATHERLOVE.

Moses once asked a burning bush, *"Who shall I tell them sent me?"*

The bush replied, "I AM—tell them I AM sent you."

Change the words "I Am" to "FATHERLOVE."
"Who shall I tell them sent me?"
"FATHERLOVE—tell them FATHERLOVE sent you."

Love is the Ultimate Ethic in Heaven and on Earth

God does not only have LOVE to share and give. God is LOVE; LOVE is GOD. We, as God's *creation, possess* LOVE. It is not just some substance or "cologne" we put on for our advantage when the situation suits us. No! We *possess* LOVE because we are *"made in the image of God"* and that *image* is LOVE. God's LOVE DNA is inside of us—our spirits feel its warmth and tenderness. Without FATHERLOVE, the best we can know of LOVE is what the world has to offer. The absolute, very *best* the world has to offer does not come close to approaching the smallest sample of FATHERLOVE in our life. The Holy Spirit imparts a sampling HE calls *"fruit":*

> But the fruit produced by the Holy Spirit
> within you is divine love in all its varied expressions:
> joy that overflows,
> peace that subdues,
> patience that endures,
> kindness in action,
> a life full of virtue,
> faith that prevails, gentleness of heart, and
> strength of spirit. Never set the law above
> these qualities, for they are meant to be limitless.
> (Galatians 5:22–23 TPT)

These are not the *joy, peace, patience, kindness, virtue, faith, gentleness, and strength* that the world can give or that we can earn or learn on our own. These are the *supernatural* gifts of LOVE from the TRIUNE GODHEAD that only the Holy Spirit can impart to us, the kind of overwhelming, consuming JOY that made Paul and Silas *laugh and sing* after being brutally beaten and thrown into a dirty, wet prison hole, the type of PEACE that completely covers you with contentment when all is *turmoil and upheaval* around you, the kind of STRENGTH that endures and sustains you when you can *barely stand* both physically and spiritually.

The world gives *fleeting happiness*—God gives eternal JOY. The world gives *rest for a season*—God gives shalom *peace* transforming the heart. The world gives *controlled tolerance*—God gives compassionate *patience and kindness*. The world gives *doubt and distrust*—God gives *deep-rooted faith* and *truth*. The world gives *depression' and guilt*—God gives *hope* and *strength*.

These are all *expressions* of FATHERLOVE.

Do not live by your *feelings* as *feelings* tend to be *fleeting and fickle*.

LOVE is not *fickle*.

LOVE is not a feeling.

LOVE is a choice—GOD *chose* to LOVE YOU! HE did not have to—and HE had every right not to. But HE did

- because HE LOVES YOU SO MUCH!
- because HE is our FATHER!

And that is why GOD is FATHERLOVE.

CHAPTER 8

GOD'S PLAN

We have the *Diary*—God's Holy Spirit inspired Word—that reveals God's *mind* and the *heart* for His *Intention* with creation. We know the *Diary* is our key to unlocking and understanding the *"hidden mystery"* of God's *Purpose* and *Plan* for creation.

It is an old *Diary*, began over 3,500 years ago, written in three ancient languages—Old Hebrew, Arabic, and Koine Greek. Translation of the documents is a very delicate and often tricky endeavor. There are no originals, only copies of copies of copies made over centuries while empires, holy men, and belief systems came and went, many attempting to influence the translations. The ancient Hebrew written language used no vowels or punctuation and was read from right to left, beginning at the back of the Book.

Translation depends upon two basic foundations: the words used and the context in which they are used. Like English, many words have multiple meanings, and the translator's task is to determine which meaning applies to each situation. The context of a term used in an ancient cultural setting can be exceedingly difficult to ascertain. But language science has significantly advanced and can achieve remarkable results in determining word usage. Understanding the context requires understanding the cultures of the age in question, word usages, and idioms. Interpretations can vary significantly based upon the culture. For example, for someone to write that it was a "gay" time in 1950 would carry a completely different meaning than when written in 2020.

Modern Bible scholars and commentators are at the mercy of translators. The good news is that an increasing number of excellent translators are emerging on the scene, capable and dedicated to their art. As a result, there is a growing number of excellent references, dictionaries, and concordances available for "students" to dig into.

Along with the Internet, there is no shortage of *tools* to research and investigate *Diary* notations in conjunction with *secular and cultural history*. Such is the case with our quest to determine what was in the mind and heart of God when He decided to make creation. We find answers we are looking for in both the *Diary* and in *recorded cultural history*.

A Two-Word Stumbling Block

Over the centuries, two words have created confusion, causing Christians to stumble in their quest to understanding God's *Ultimate Purpose and Plan* with creation.

Two words have been misinterpreted, misunderstood, and misapplied due to questionable translation choices, coupled with a lack of first-century cultural understanding.

The problem and resultant confusion from these two words does not come from the writer's error but the translator's poor choice of interpretations. The words we are concerned with are found in the New Testament portion of the *Diary* and are therefore translated from the *ancient Koine Greek* language.

Koine Greek,[5] also known as *Alexandrian dialect* and *Hellenistic Greek*, was a common form of *Attic Greek* spoken and written during the New Testament period. It evolved following Alexander the Great's conquests across the known world to enable trade and civil obedience among the various nations within the Greek Empire. When the Roman Empire replaced the Greek Empire, Koine Greek was established, and the Romans left it in place to serve their purposes. The *Septuagint*[6] is the *Tanakh* (Hebrew Bible) translated into *Koine Greek*, done hundreds of years before Jesus walked the earth. This was the

---

[5] https://en.wikipedia.org/wiki/Koine_Greek.

[6] https://en.wikipedia.org/wiki/Septuagint.

primary source of Scriptures used during Jesus's lifetime. The majority (possibly all) of the New Testament was written in *Koine Greek*.

In addition to translation from *Koine Greek*, to interpret New Testament Scripture, it must be read and understood from the author's first-century viewpoint and not from either a thirteenth-century translator's perspective or our twenty-first-century viewpoint.

One of the reasons many believers miss God's *Ultimate Purpose and Plan* is that both of the explosive words we are referring to are used together in our foundational Scripture and are critical to our understanding of it. Let us refresh ourselves with that *Diary* entry once again:

> *Just as He chose us in Him before the foundation of the world, that we would be holy and blameless before Him. In love He predestined us to adoption as sons and daughters through Jesus Christ to Himself, according to the good pleasure of His will... In all wisdom and insight, He made known to us the mystery of His will, according to His good pleasure which He set forth in Him, regarding His plan of the fullness of the times, to bring all things together in Christ, things in the heavens and things on the earth. In Him we also have obtained an inheritance, having been predestined according to the purpose of Him who works all things in accordance with the plan of His will.* (Ephesians 1:4–11 NASB)

The First Explosive Word

Christianity has seen much debate, confusion, and disagreement, as well as out and out hostility, dissension, ex-communication, and physical warfare, over the definition of this word!

What word has created such a whirlwind within Christianity? *Predestination.*

Denominations have split down the middle on the issue, splintering into battle lines of *predestination* versus *free will*. Christian doctrines and thought patterns have become entrenched and solidified, defending either the Calvinistic or the Armenian viewpoint. Interestingly, this was not an issue within the church until hundreds of years following Jesus's ascension, but it has been one ever since.

We certainly do not wish to add any fuel to those fires, and our prayer is that our loving Father will give us revelation to still and quiet this divisive beast for the sake of our quest here. What we do want to do is to understand the context and usage of the word in the Apostle Paul's letters to know how the word applies to God's *Ultimate Purpose and Plan* with creation.

To do so, we ask the reader to put aside any preconceived thoughts regarding *predestination* from other *Scripture usages and doctrines*. Just look at what the Holy Spirit shows Paul with this particular usage of the word. For our study, we will look strictly at how the word itself is defined and used in *this situation* only and avoid getting into doctrinal definitions of where and how it is used elsewhere.

First, let us understand how the word is defined and understood in our modern age by the secular world. According to *Webster, predestination* is defined as

> Predestination[7]—<u>noun</u>
> 1. the action of God in foreordaining from eternity whatever comes to pass.
> 2. the doctrine that God, in consequence of his foreknowledge of all events, infallibly guides those destined for salvation.
> 3. The doctrine of Calvinist and other beliefs that God has determined from eternity those to be saved or damned regardless of merit or actions.
>
> First Known Use: 14th century, in the meanings defined above.

---

[7] https://www.merriam-webster.com/dictionary/predestination.

One thing that makes this word difficult to translate is that it is similar to many English words. It can have different definitions depending on the context in which it is used. For example,

And these whom He predestined, He also called; and these whom He called, He also justified; and these whom He justified, He also glorified. (Romans 8:30 NASB)

We are sure Paul is thinking of himself in the above statement as he was selectively "called" by the Lord to be His Apostle to the Gentiles. Paul believes God selectively chose him for the task he was assigned, which very well is probably true. But applying that definition across the board in all uses of the word can create some serious misunderstandings.

It is easy to see how applying this definition to Paul's letter to the Ephesians can lead us into a quagmire of confusion and disagreement. We will not touch on this definition as we do not see it in this context.

Interpreting Predestination

To interpret our phrase, we need to get away from the translator's chosen English word—*predestination*—and go directly to the actual Greek word used by Paul.

That Greek word is *pro'orizo*.[8] It is a compound word and is defined in *Strong's Expanded Exhaustive Concordance of the Bible*; number 4309, as follows:

> *pro*—meaning: *before*,
> and
> *horizo*—meaning: *define the limits of; to set boundaries of.*

Horizo is where we get the English word *horizon* from, so you can see the idea conveyed of *setting* the limits or boundaries of something. For example, the *horizon* is the physical *boundary limit* that our vision can see.

---

8   https://biblehub.com/greek/4309.htm; http://www.graceandtruth.net/images/
    stories/docs/articles/Notes%20predestination%202011-01-13%20(1).pdf.

Compounded, the word means

> *to determine the boundaries or limits of something beforehand. To determine boundaries and limits of something to make a PLAN!*

Paul is telling us that this is a *Plan* God decided to make *beforehand*—before creation!

Consider *Webster's* secular definition of *predestine* as a verb:

Predestine[9]—<u>verb</u>

> *to destine, decree, determine, appoint, or settle beforehand.*

This modern definition of the verb form of *predestine* is almost identical to the ancient Greek definition of *pro'orizo!* Is it conceivable that translators used the *noun* definition and should have used the *verb* definition?

What is important is that we know just what *pro'orizo* meant to Paul and his audience when he used the word two thousand years ago. That is the only definition that matters.

The *Pro'orizo*

To understand Paul's usage, we first need to determine what that *something* is that God is setting boundaries or making a *Plan* for? In our *Foundational Scripture* of Ephesians, the word *Pro'orizo* precedes *"adoption."* Hence, the context is that God established *the boundaries of a plan* for someone to be *adopted.* Who is that *someone?* The *someone* is *us*, so it is a plan for *us* to be *adopted. Adopted* as what? Continue reading: *"as sons and daughters through Jesus Christ to Himself."*

Here it is! Clear and with no room for misinterpretation. *Before God created anything, He made a plan whereby people (us) could be adopted to Himself as sons and daughters, through Jesus Christ!*

---

9 https://www.merriam-webster.com/dictionary/predestine.

Reading the entire passage, within this *plan*, God would have *"sons and daughters"* that He would *adopt* into His *Family*, strictly for His enjoyment. In other words, it was God's *Ultimate Intention* to have a family, and He laid out a plan—*set the boundaries of*—on how that would happen, through His Beloved Son, Jesus Christ. *That is what He desired to accomplish with creation.* That is what He wanted to end up with.

> *He predestined to be conformed to the image*
> *of His Son so that He might be the firstborn among*
> *many brothers.* (Romans 8:29 MEV)

In other words, what was *predestined* or *predetermined* was the *what*—the plan—not the *who* (the sons and daughters). It shows no connection to individual people receiving salvation but instead connects to people being adopted. In this context, Paul is not saying He *"predetermined"* that Bobby and Sue would go to heaven, and Bill and Sally would go to hell. Paul is saying that God *"predetermined"* a plan whereby Bobby, Sue, Bill, and Sally would have the opportunity to join the FATHER FAMILY, in the Kingdom of God, by being transformed into the image of His *Beloved* Son, Jesus, through *adoption*. God desires that *all* should come to repentance and be in His Kingdom and not only some *preselected* few. And He knows, by *foreknowledge* of the view from His "celestial helicopter," who would accept and who would not. But the choice to do so or not *was theirs*—their *free will* to accept or reject the Father. Some may take exception to this, and that is their prerogative, but looking at the words used and the context and knowing that the desire of God is for *all* to come to Him, this understanding is clear, simple, and expresses the *heart* of the FATHER. We are not making any statement regarding the Calvinistic or the Armenian viewpoints either way as we do not see that as Paul's issue in this context. We are only speaking of God's *Plan* as presented here.

Interpreted as a noun, the translator's use of *predestination* does not fully convey Paul's message. But as a verb, it does. The difference between a noun and a verb, in this context, is night and day.

In his letter to Corinth, Paul revealed having an *"out of body"* experience where he was taken to the third heaven. The stage was set—the *prophecies fulfilled*—the Messiah had come; the LORD JESUS CHRIST had bridged the error of the *first Adam* and had reconnected our pathway into the presence of God to fulfill His *Ultimate Purpose and Plan* of creation. The HOLY SPIRIT had been released to all *who would believe and accept* salvation and redemption, by unmerited favor and grace, and who would spend eternity in the KINGDOM OF GOD.

The time had come for the mystery of what was God's ORIGINAL INTENTION with creation to be unveiled.

Paul *was chosen* to unveil the *"mystery."* What an honor he was given! For thousands of years, God had put His *pro'orizo (predetermined plan)* in place leading up to this pivotal moment in history! All the patriarchs (Adam, Abraham, Moses, David), the mighty prophets (Elijah, Elisha, Ezekiel, and Daniel) had come and gone, each playing a part, each seeing a role, but none seeing the whole. Like viewing the parade, each only seeing that small portion passing in front of them. But now, FATHER is taking the Apostle Paul for a ride in His "celestial helicopter" and showing him the whole parade, from start to finish, so that Paul can reveal to the world just what is and has been God's *Intention* all along.

And we get to share in this great revelation! *Do not ever think God does not love you!*

In the letters he wrote to Rome, Ephesus, Colossi, and Philippi, Paul presents this *astonishing revelation*. It is all there—all we must do is put the pieces together. What an honor we have today to be able to see into the heart of FATHERLOVE, chosen and placed at this time in history with our FATHER, not only by faith *but by sight*, having been shown the FATHER's heart, and being a part of its fulfillment!

It is a marvelous revelation, and Paul can hardly contain himself in presenting it. Paul's letter to the church at Ephesus clearly and abundantly reveals FATHERLOVE's desire:

> *That the God of our Lord Jesus Christ, the*
> *Father of glory, may give to you the spirit of wisdom*

and revelation in the knowledge of Him, the eyes of
your understanding being enlightened; that you may
know what is the hope of His calling, what are the
riches of the glory of His inheritance in the saints,
and what is the exceeding greatness of His power
toward us who believe, according to the working of
His mighty power. (Ephesians 1:17–19 NKJV)

The letter overflows with this enlightened and exhilarating mystery. The words vibrate and are unconstrained in joy at the *Good News* that we are created to share in the *glory* and *splendor* of the Kingdom of God on earth alongside His begotten Son, Jesus Christ! Please read all of this letter and his letters to the other Ekklesias, where each one focuses on another part of the revelation. His letter to the Ekklesia at Colossi reveals the central focus of FATHER's *pro'orizo*—His Beloved Son, *Yeshua HaMashiach*—*Jesus the Messiah.* His letter to the Ekklesia in Rome details the nation of *Israel's role, the fall of man off the path, his salvation and justification* back onto the path. Paul's letters to the Ekklesias at *Philippi, Galatia, Corinth,* and *Ephesus* expound on the adoption process. Further revelations on the FATHER's ULTIMATE INTENTION are given to the writer of HEBREWS and to John on the Isle of Patmos.

The mystery which has been hidden from ages
and from generations, but now has been revealed to
His saints. (Colossians 1:26 NKJV)

The Revelation of Jesus Christ, which God
gave Him to show His servants—things which must
shortly take place. And He sent and signified it by His
angel to His servant John. (Revelation 1:1 NKJV)

Before anything was, before He spoke the universe into existence, the Triune God established His *plan.* He created man *"in His image"* to be a significant participant in that plan, and He sent and planted His Son, JESUS CHRIST—the *second Adam*—right into the middle of it to make it all work. It is an eternal, glorious plan of living with FATHERLOVE—in all His glory!

> *In Him also we have obtained an inheritance,*
> *being predestined (planned) according to the pur-*
> *pose of Him who works all things according to the*
> *counsel of His will.* (Ephesians 1:11 NKJV)

It is a *Plan* for His creation to share, bask, and live with FATHERLOVE! FATHER would have a family—a *family* of sons and daughters, centered *on, about, with, through,* and *in* Jesus—joyfully, excitedly, and happily *sharing* in the vast greatness of God's *freely given, undeserved mercy, grace, and inheritance!*

How glorious! How magnificent! FATHERLOVE loves HIS CHILDREN so much that HE put all this into place so that we could *share it* with HIM! What an unbelievable plan! Thank You, FATHER, for being so great, so loving, so caring for Your children. Thank You! You are indeed a Good FATHER.

Jesus knew the plan. He went to all the towns and villages teaching the Gospel of the Kingdom of God. The *plan* is what Jesus fulfilled in the world—the *plan* of the Kingdom.

> *But seek first the kingdom of God and His*
> *righteousness.* (Matthew 6:33 NKJV)

When facing the cross, knowing His hour had come, this is what Jesus prayed:

> *And now, O Father, glorify Me together with*
> *Yourself, with the glory which I had with You before*
> *the world was… And the glory which You gave Me*
> *I have given them, that they may be one just as We*
> *are one: I in them, and You in Me; that they may be*
> *made perfect in one, and that the world may know*
> *that You have sent Me, and have loved them as You*
> *have loved Me.* (John 17:5, 22–23 NKJV)

What a marvelous plan from a magnificent God who loves us so much! That plan would consist of children who would willingly come to Him and whom He would take in as "*sons,*" in the image of Christ, and who would share the inheritance of the Kingdom.

The template of the plan was shown to Isaiah the Prophet more than seven hundred years before Jesus walked the earth when he prophesied the coming of the Messiah—the *firstborn*:

> *For unto us a Child is born, unto us, a Son is given; And the government will be upon His shoulder. And His name will be called Wonderful, Counselor, Mighty God, Everlasting Father, Prince of Peace.* (Isaiah 9:6 MEV)

And the prophecy was fulfilled:

> *But when the fullness of the time came, God sent forth His Son, born of a woman, born under the Law, so that He might redeem those who were under the Law, that we might receive the adoption as sons.* (Galatians 4:4–5 MEV)

Let us not allow ourselves to get "off track" by a translator's word usage and miss the understanding of the Father's *Original Intention* with creation. His plan is too precious—too wonderful—for us to overlook by getting lost in doctrinal disputes. Whether one believes in Calvinism or Armenian, FATHERLOVE made this plan for both of you—for you and for me—because He loves us so much. He wants us to share and extend His love outward—throughout the universe—for all of eternity!

Let us just rejoice and say, "*Thank You, Father.*"

CHAPTER 9

BORN FOR ADOPTION

From an "*out of body experience,*" the Apostle Paul had, we have learned that God's *Ultimate Intention, Purpose, and Plan* with creation was to create a "family" of "*sons and daughters*" who would "co-inherit" the Kingdom of God through and with *Yeshua HaMashiach—Jesus the Messiah.*

> *Just as He chose us in Him before the foundation of the world, that we would be holy and blameless before Him. In love, He predestined us to adoption as sons and daughters through Jesus Christ to Himself, according to the good pleasure of His will.* (Ephesians 1:4–6 NASB)

To the Galatians, Paul expounded on becoming "adopted" sons of the kingdom:

> *Now I say, as long as the heir is a child, he does not differ at all from a slave although he is owner of everything…that we might receive the adoption as sons… Therefore you are no longer a slave, but a son; and if a son, then an heir through God.* (Galatians 4:1, 3–7 NASB)

*But what does this mean—"adoption"? Did
not Jesus say we must be "born again"?*

*Jesus answered and said to him, "Truly, truly,
I say to you, unless one is BORN AGAIN, he cannot see
the kingdom of God." (John 3:3 NASB)*

*Jesus answered, "Truly, truly, I say to you,
unless one is born of water and the Spirit he cannot
enter into the kingdom of God. That which is born
of the flesh is flesh, and that which is born of the
Spirit is spirit. Do not be amazed that I said to you,
'You must be born again.'" (John 3:5–7 NASB)*

Now a decade after Jesus ascended to the Father, the Apostle
Paul is telling us that the *Plan* is for us to be *adopted* into God's *family*. Being *adopted* into a family is totally different from being *born*
into a family. Is this not in conflict with what our Lord told us? Is
Paul teaching a new salvation message from Christ? Are there two
ways to salvation—*"born again"* and *"adoption"*?

Some say, *"It's just a play on words. It doesn't make any difference."*
Others say, *"Paul misunderstood what the Spirit was showing him."*

Because it is stated in God's *Ultimate Intention, Purpose, and
Plan* for creation, we need to understand precisely what it means.
Maybe it is just a *play on words*, and then again, maybe it is not. But
seeing that it is specifically pointed out as an intricate part of God's
Purpose and Plan for creation, a little investigation and research are
called for. Whichever it is—a *play on words* or a *misinterpretation* or
if it is exactly what is meant—we need to know.

If *"adoption"* is the word Paul meant to use, then we need to
answer the question: *Are we "born again," or are we "adopted"?*

"Born Again" or "Adopted"?

Recall in the previous chapter. We said there are two words
that have created great confusion and discussion within the ranks

of Christianity. We discussed the first of those words, being *predestination*.

Yes, you guessed it, the second word is *adoption*. As we said, both of these controversial words are used together in our Foundational Scripture of Ephesians from the *Diary*. Let us refresh again:

> *In love He predestined us to adoption as sons and daughters through Jesus Christ to Himself, according to the good pleasure of His will...predestined according to the purpose of Him who works all things in accordance with the plan of His will.* (Ephesians 1:5, 11 NASB)

But before we explore what the Apostle Paul meant by saying God's plan is for us to be *"adopted as sons and daughters,"* let us not have any confusion regarding our salvation.

If there is anything explicitly clear in Scripture, it is that our salvation comes by being *"born again"* as children of God. Into God's *Family*, entrance into the Kingdom of God, is by birth, by being *"born again."* Jesus was explicit, *"You MUST be born again."* And we are *"born again"* by believing and accepting Jesus Christ as our Savior and Lord.

It needs to be crystal clear, without any confusion, salvation is not given by *adoption*. It is the free gift of God, unearned, unmerited, given by *grace* alone, causing us to be *"born again"* into the kingdom of God.

What is "Predestined" for "Adoption"?

So then, what is *"Adoption"* all about that the Apostle Paul tells us is God's *Plan* for us from the beginning of time? If I am *"born again,"* how and why and by whom do I get *"adopted"*?

Interestingly, of all the New Testament writers, only Paul spoke of *adoption*, and then only in five verses in his letters to the churches (of course, Paul is the only one who had the *"out of body"* experience that we are aware of).

Once to the *Ekklesias* in Galatia:

> *But when the fullness of the time came, God sent forth His Son, born of a woman, born under the Law, so that He might redeem those who were under the Law, that we might receive the adoption as sons.* (Galatians 4:4–5 MEV)

Once to the *Ekklesia* at Ephesus:

> *He predestined us to adoption as sons through Jesus Christ to Himself, according to the kind intention of His will.* (Ephesians 1:5 NASB)

And three times to the *Ekklesias* in Rome:

> *For you have not received a spirit of slavery leading to fear again, but you have received a spirit of adoption as sons by which we cry out, "Abba! Father!"* (Romans 8:15 NASB)

> *And not only this but also, we ourselves, having the first fruits of the Spirit, even we ourselves groan within ourselves, waiting eagerly for our adoption as sons, the redemption of our body.* (Romans 8:23 NASB)

> *For I could wish that I myself were accursed, separated from Christ for the sake of my brethren, my kinsmen according to the flesh, who are Israelites, to whom belongs the adoption as sons, and the glory and the covenants and the giving of the Law and the temple service and the promises.* (Romans 9:3–4 NASB)

In our modern Western thought, the concept of *adoption* is for people, usually a couple, to acquire a baby. They make a legal request, and after some background checks, money exchange, and paper signings, they are presented with a child, usually a baby, born of some other woman, usually a stranger. The baby is accepted into the family as if it had been physically born into the adopted family.

If we are going to understand the word *adoption* as it applies to God's *Ultimate Purpose and Plan* for us, then we must remove our preconceived modern-day concept of *adoption* and view it from the first-century concept of *Adoption* that the Apostle Paul was speaking from and to.

Paul was a Jew, a Pharisee from the tribe of Benjamin, so what was the Jewish concept of *adoption*? Well, it appears that a word for *adoption* did not even exist in the Hebrew language at that time. There is no mention of any word meaning *adoption* in the Tanakh (Hebrew Bible), and there was no process for *adoption* in the ancient Jewish culture. A person's standing as an Israelite was based on their tribal birth. There was no such thing as "moving" from one tribe to another. If a man died without children, his brother was required to marry the widow. The first son to be born of the new marriage would be legally considered the son of the dead brother to continue his family tribal name.

Outside persons could join into a tribe, but there were little formal means for that to occur, and they didn't hold all the same rights birth tribal members held. They would "attach" themselves, like Ruth: "*Where you go, I will go.*" There was more ceremony for entry into Judaism than into the tribal nationality.

Therefore, we can safely say that Paul is not speaking of Hebrew *adoption*, seeing that there essentially was none for him to speak of.

So what is he speaking about?

We must not forget that Paul was also a Roman citizen who grew up in Tarsus, a prominent Roman crossroads and an educational epicenter of the Empire. Also notice who his audiences are when using the term *adoption,* the people of Ephesus, Galatia, and Rome—*Gentile citizens of the Roman Empire.* Paul is speaking to them of a concept that he does not explain, so it is obviously a concept they understood. Once again, let us look at the Greek wording he actually used and not some translator's chosen English word.

That word is *huio'thesia*.[10] It is a compound word consisting of *huios*, which means "*a son,*" and *tithemi*, defined as "*to set, place, or to put in place.*" Combined, the word *huio'thesia* incorporates the entire translated phrase of "*adoption as sons.*"

In *Strong's Exhaustive Concordance of the Bible*, *huio'thesia* is defined as

> *the dignity of the relationship as sons; it is NOT of putting into a family by birth, but of putting into the position of sons for inheritance* (emphasis mine).

Huio'thesia did not focus on adding a child to the "family," but it dealt with the issue of "family" *inheritance*. Roman *huio'thesia* aimed at providing a suitable male heir for a Roman citizen's property and wealth to transfer. The word carried a distinct and very understood meaning in the first-century Roman Empire and was considered a *badge of honor*.

In our world, we write *wills* and leave our property to anyone we want, male or female, young or old, family member or not. That was not the case in the ancient Roman world; wherewith few exceptions, a man passed his wealth on to his *son*. Due to constant wars, empire expansion, and poor health, male life expectancy was less than 50 percent after the age of eighteen. If a man had no sons or felt that his sons were either incapable of managing his property or unworthy of receiving his wealth, he could select someone else who would make a worthy *son*. These selections were not infant *adoptions* as we think of today as adult men were chosen, many times older than the person doing the selecting.

---

[10] https://en.wikipedia.org/wiki/Adoption_in_ancient_Rome
http://concernedbrothers.com/truth/huiothesia.pdf
https://www2.gracenotes.info/topics/adoption.pdf.

The high mortality and short longevity rates among the Roman Empire population resulted in *huio'thesia* being a fairly common practice, especially among the *upper* classes.

Unbelievable as it may appear, when a child was born biologically, the parents had the option of disowning the child and offering it to the "gods" for a variety of reasons. If not desired by the parent, the relationship of a birth child was not permanent and could be terminated easily. On the other hand, *huio'thesia* was permanent and could not be terminated!

The *huio'thesia* Process

Huio'thesia carried great weight and had a powerful meaning. In Roman culture, the father held total control over the family. This was termed *pater familias*.[11] If a father chose a person for *huio'thesia*, the person had to relinquish all claim and title to his original *pater familias* (father family) and come under the total control of his *new* father.

When a person was brought on by *huio'thesia,* it meant:

- That person was freely chosen by the father, who openly paid the price for him to join his family.
- That person would be a fully participating part of the family.
- That person received a new identity.
- Any prior commitments, responsibilities, and debts were erased.
- New rights and responsibilities were taken on.
- Inheritance was part of life, not something that began at death.
- Being *huio'thesia* made someone an heir to their father and wholly united to him.
- The person switched from the control of his former *pater familias* to the authority of his adoptive *pater familias*.

---

[11] https://en.wikipedia.org/wiki/Pater_familias.

- A father could disown his natural-born son, but *huiothesia* was permanent and irreversible.

Huiothesia was not completed in one step, as modern *adoption* is, but consisted of two formal stages. The first was called the *mancipatio*, and it consisted of purchasing the person by the father.

The person selected was then placed under the authority of a tutor who, in addition to instruction and maturing, had full authority to discipline the person. Keep in mind, these were not children but were fully grown adults. The new member was practically in a "slave" status to the tutor, whose responsibility was to transform the "new" family member into a mature, active, worthy "son" of the Father, capable of carrying on the "family" name.

The second stage was a formal ceremony called *vindicatio*. When the "son" was ready, the father went to the Roman authorities to advocate for legal acceptance of the person to receive the father's inheritance. Upon legal approval, the person would receive a new cloak and a new name. He would be the legal son of his new father and entitled to the father's inheritance. This is important: the father was not declaring that the person was now a member of his family—he had already accepted, purchased, and declared the person as a "member" of the family during the first phase. He was announcing to the world that the person was now a "mature son," capable of managing the father's wealth, property, and affairs, and that from this point on, others must accept the person the same as they would accept the father.

If the "son" now needed any further discipline, the tutor may no longer give it. He was no longer in a "slave" status but was now a "mature" master of the house. Disobedience and discipline were now between the son and the father.

An excellent example of *huiothesia* is presented in the novel titled *Ben-Hur: A Tale of the Christ*[12] by Lew Wallace.

---

[12] https://en.wikipedia.org/wiki/Ben-Hur:_A_Tale_of_the_Christ#:~:text=Ben-Hur%.

Recall in the movie version of the story, when *Judah Ben-Hur* (Charlton Heston), a Jewish slave on a Roman war galley, saves the Roman commander's life, Arrius, who had attempted suicide, thinking the battle had been lost. But the battle was a victory, and resultantly, Arrius was returning as a "hero" to Rome. He pardons Judah of his "crimes" and *adopts* him as his son. During the ceremony, Judah Ben-Hur is given Arrius's signet ring, a new name (*Young Arrius*), and all the family's inheritance rights.

Judah Ben-Hur proclaims, *"I have been given a new life, a new home, and a new father."*

History provides numerous real-life examples of *huio'thesia* from ancient Rome. A most interesting one (and quite ironic, seeing that he is the person who had the Apostle Paul beheaded for preaching *adoption* within God's family!) is Emperor Nero.

Nero was not in the then Emperor Claudius's family lineage, but Nero wanted to become emperor. So Claudius *adopted*[13] Nero so that Nero might succeed him on the throne. Here is where it gets interesting: Claudius had a daughter, Octavia. Nero decided to marry Octavia as well. Of course, Nero and Octavia were in no way brother and sister, not blood related by any means. But in the eyes of the law, due to Nero's *adoption* by Claudius, they were brother and sister; and were forbidden to marry. Nero bribed the Roman Senate to pass special legislation to enable him to marry Octavia.

So you see, *huio'thesia* was real—final and binding.

Paul, writing to Roman audiences, uses the word *huio'thesia*, which his Roman audiences would clearly have understood the meaning of without any hesitation.

So what is Paul saying to us?

What does this mean to our understanding of Ephesians 1:4?

It means that "*adoption*" is not the best word to be used in connection with *huio'thesia*. Translation of the word as *adoption* is a poor choice of words. A better choice would be *"gaining an inheritance."*

---

[13] https://en.wikipedia.org/wiki/Adoption_in_ancient_Rome.

The word has everything to do with becoming mature and gaining inheritance within a new family.

We could paraphrase our foundational Scriptures as follows:

> *In love He made a plan for us to coinherit, as sons and daughters, through Jesus Christ to Himself, according to the good pleasure of His will.* (Ephesians 1:5, 11 paraphrased)

> *But when the fullness of the time came, God sent forth His Son, born of a woman, born under the Law, so that He might redeem those who were under the Law, that we might receive the inheritance as sons.* (Galatians 4:45 paraphrased)

> *For you have not received a spirit of slavery leading to fear again, but you have received a spirit of inheritance as sons by which we cry out, "Abba! Father!"* (Romans 8:15 paraphrased)

> *And not only this but also, we ourselves, having the first fruits of the Spirit, even we ourselves groan within ourselves, waiting eagerly for our inheritance as sons, the redemption of our body.* (Romans 8:23 paraphrased)

> *For I could wish that I myself were accursed, separated from Christ for the sake of my brethren, my kinsmen according to the flesh, who are Israelites, to who belongs the inheritance as sons, and the glory and the covenants and the giving of the Law and the temple service and the promises.* (Romans 9:3–4 paraphrased)

Each step of Roman *adoption* is meaningful and applicable to our Christian walk.

When a person accepts Jesus Christ as their Lord and Savior, they are *"born again"* and enter into the *family* of God. This is akin to *manci'patio*, the first step of the *adoption* process. The Father has purchased him and welcomes him into His *Pater familias*—His Father Family.

The person did nothing to earn it—he does not deserve it. It is only by the great MERCY, GRACE, and LOVE of the Father that he is given it. The old *pater familias* (satan and the world) has no more power or rights over him. He begins a new life. His old life is erased; his debts are canceled—his sins are forgiven. He gains all the rights of a fully legitimate child in his new Father's family.

The purchase price paid by the Father?

The Blood of His only Begotten Son—Jesus Christ!

Like the Roman *adoption,* the new family member is put under the tutorage of a "teacher" responsible for teaching, nurturing, counseling, guiding, and disciplining him into family maturity.

In our walk with Christ, when we are *"born again,"* we are given a tutor to teach, nurture, counsel, guide, and discipline us to into maturity. That tutor is the Holy Spirit.

> *Nevertheless, I tell you the truth: It is expedient for you that I go away. For if I do not go away, the Counselor will not come to you. But if I go, I will send Him to you. When He comes, He will convict the world of sin and of righteousness and of judgment... I have yet many things to tell you, but you cannot bear them now. But when the Spirit of truth comes, He will guide you into all truth. For He will not speak on His own authority. But He will speak whatever He hears, and He will tell you things that are to come. (John 16:7–12 MEV)*

> *But the Helper, the Holy Spirit, whom the Father will send in My name, He will teach you all things, and bring to your remembrance all that I said to you. (John 14:26 NKJV)*

We mature. We learn of God's Plan and Purpose. Through the counsel and wisdom of the Holy Spirit, we undergo a transformation from *self-centered* carnal beings to *God-centered* mighty "sons and daughters" of God, modeled and molded in the image of Jesus Christ.

As long as we retain our fleshly bodies, we fall short of achieving full maturity. It is at the rapture of God's saints from all time that God will receive His "sons and daughters"—His *Ekklesia*—to Himself. That day will see the completion of the second Step—the *vindi'catio*—where we will receive our "graduation diplomas," our resurrected glorified bodies!

We will then have the authority as His sons to rule and reign with Him in His Kingdom. We will go from being the *"children of God"* to being the *"sons and daughters of God."*

Huio'thesia was not an unwelcomed status for the people of the Roman Empire. Instead, it was a coveted status, offered freely, to join the family and potentially rule the Roman Empire with him. There was nothing more joyful for a common person than to discover that he was being offered *adoption* by a powerful Roman family and would have his past erased. His future is secured with the inheritance of the father.

Likewise, *adoption* is not an unwelcome status for the people of this world's kingdom. It too is a coveted status, offered freely in love by a loving FATHER, to join His *Family* and potentially rule the Kingdom of God with Him. There is nothing more joyful than for a sinner to discover he is offered *adoption* by the Creator and have his past erased and his future secured with the inheritance of FATHERLOVE.

Knowing the meaning of *huio'thesia*, which gloried in Roman power, illuminates the *Ultimate Intention* of God—to create a family of sons and daughters who glorify in God's power and love. The grace of *adoption* is afforded to us as slaves of sin, offering us citizenship in God's Kingdom, not as slaves but through the council and tutorage of the Holy Spirit as *"sons and daughters"*—coheirs with Christ.

So back to our two questions:

First, *Isn't it just a play on words? What does it matter anyway?*

As we see, it is not a *play on words,* and there is a vast difference between being "born again" and being "adopted," the difference between a child wearing diapers and dependent on milk feedings and a fully grown, mature man. From the Scriptures in Ephesians and Colossians, it is clear that God's *Plan* is for men and women to be brought into the kingdom and grow, learn, and advance into capable, mature "*sons and daughters*" who can become "coheirs" with Jesus Christ. God's *Plan* does not stop at *salvation,* but rather, salvation is the beginning of the journey to fulfill God's *Ultimate Purpose and Plan* with creation.

Secondly, *Which is it? Are we born again or are we adopted?*

The answer is, *we are born again into God's Kingdom to be tutored and nurtured to achieve adoption as mature sons and daughters, to be coheirs of the Kingdom of God through and with Jesus Christ.*

In other words, *we are born again to be adopted.*

What a great plan! And why?

For no other reason than He loves us so.

CHAPTER 10

"UNTO US A SON"

"When I was a child"

In our journey thus far, we have seen that Jesus told us we "*must be born again*," and the Apostle Paul revealed that God's plan was for His "*born again*" children to be "*adopted*" as mature "*sons*" and "*coheirs*" with Christ of the Kingdom.

In the *Diary,* the terms "*child of God*" and "*son of God*" are used repeatedly, and as such, it is implied that they are synonymous with no distinction between them. Many commentators, authors, and ministers have used those two terms interchangeably. Is that correct? Do they mean the same thing, or is that taking liberty with semantics? This is a critical concern as it is a key element to understanding God's *Purpose and Plan* and one which needs to be grounded on a solid Scriptural foundation. Are they, in fact, interchangeable? Or do they carry different meanings? As we proceed on our quest, it not only would be worthwhile but necessary to examine them.

Within the New Testament writings, there are numerous Greek words used to designate "*children*." Most of these refer to a young child or a group of young children.

When used in the context of "*believers*" in Christ, there are four words mostly used in Scripture, with two of them used repeatedly in describing *believers* as grown children—*teknon* and *huios*. Let us look at all four of them.

Nepios

This word, used sparingly, refers to an *immature* or *gullible* Christian. It is used by Paul when exhorting believers to higher and deeper understandings of the Gospel of the Kingdom and not to be led astray by false teachings.

> *That we should no longer be children (nepios), tossed to and from and carried about with every wind of doctrine, by the trickery of men, in the cunning craftiness of deceitful plotting.* (Ephesians 4:14)

Paidon

It is used to describe a small or young child, 2–4 years of age. It is used by Paul to motivate new believers to increased understanding of the Gospel.

> *Brethren, do not be children (paidon) in understanding; however in malice be babes, but in understanding be mature.* (1 Corinthians 14:20)

Teknon and huios

The third word, *teknon*,[14] is defined according to *Strong's Concordance* number 5043 as

> *"offspring"; "the fact of birth"; "refers to a child up to his school years"*

Teknon is used indiscriminately to designate children who are maturing physically but not spiritually.

---

[14] https://www.biblehub.com/greek/5043.htm.

The fourth word, *huios*,[15] according to *Strong's Concordance* number 5207, is defined as

> *"a mature son," "stresses the quality and essence of one so resembling another that distinctions between the two are indiscernible"*

(As a point in semantics, *son* is inclusive of gender—male and female. Sorry, that was the way they talked back then. But ladies, do not feel bad. It is no different than us males being referred to as the "*bride*" of Christ.)

Huios is used indiscriminately to designate children who have grown into spiritual *maturity*.

You recall we encountered *huios* earlier as the first part of the compound word *huio'thesia*, which was translated as *"adoption of sons"* and which is interpreted as *"matured for inheritance."*

Huios is always used when describing *"spiritually mature children"* and when the speaker desired to focus on the honor, dignity, respect, and worthiness of the person being discussed.

Strong's Concordance actually makes the comparison between *teknon* and *huios* as follows:

> *Teknon gives prominence to physical and outward aspects of parentage. Huios gives prominence to the inward, ethical, legal (inheritance) aspects of parentage—the dignity and character of the relationship.*

Most translators have translated *teknon* as meaning the *"children of God"* and *huios* as the *"sons of God."* To many students of Scripture and from many pulpits, this is an exercise in semantics, and they view the two expressions as interchangeable. But as we have seen, that is not accurate; there is a difference between them, a night and day difference. On the one hand, we refer to a child being fed milk, not able

---

[15] https://biblehub.com/greek/5207.htm.

to sustain mature thinking and make mature decision. On the other hand, we are referencing a mature, thinking, capable member of the *family*, fully able and ready to participate in family affairs and receive and manage an inheritance, all the difference between a child needing nursing and constant attention and a child *growing up, maturing, learning*, and *developing* a relationship with the parents and the world around him. To interchange them as the same would be like saying one's five-year-old child is identical to their twenty-year-old child. Yes, they are both one's children, but they are totally different, having different needs, desires, duties, and separate existences.

In the Gospels, Jesus was referred to as a *brephos* (an immature infant) once, when in the manger (Luke 2:12), and as a *teknon* once, at the age of twelve years and still under His parent's tutorage (Luke 2:48).

Following this, He was referred to as the *huios* of God—more than 220 times.

God's Plan from *Teknon* to *Huios*

Knowing the meanings and cultural usage of these words gives real revelation and clarity to understanding Paul's message to the churches regarding God's *Intention, Purpose, and Plan* for us. Let us look at a few uses in Paul's Letters, beginning once again with our foundational Scripture in Ephesians:

> *Just as He chose us in Him before the foundation of the world... In love, He predestined us to adoption as sons and daughters (huios) through Jesus Christ to Himself... He made known to us the mystery of His will, according to His good pleasure which He set forth in Him, regarding His plan of the fullness of the times, bringing all things together in Christ... In Him we also have obtained an inheritance, having been predestined according to the purpose of Him who works all things in accordance with the plan of His will.* (Ephesians 1:4–11 NASB)

For as many as are led by the Spirit of God,
these are sons (huios) of God. (Romans 8:14 NKJV)

In the opening chapter of John's Gospel, we find John's explanation of being *"born again"*:

> *But as many, as received Him (Jesus), to*
> *them He gave the right to become children of God*
> *(teknon), to those who believe in His name: who*
> *were born, not of blood, nor of the will of the flesh,*
> *nor of the will of man, but of God.* (John 1:12–13
> NKJV)

Therein lies salvation—entrance into the Kingdom of GOD. Now let us look at what Paul wrote to the Galatians explaining the process that follows:

> *Now I say that the heir, as long as he is a child*
> *(teknon), does not differ at all from a slave, though*
> *he is master of all, Even so we, when we were chil-*
> *dren (teknon), were in bondage under the elements*
> *of the world. But when the fullness of the time had*
> *come, God sent forth His Son, born of a woman,*
> *born under the law, to redeem those who were under*
> *the law, that we might receive the adoption as sons*
> *(huios). And because you are sons (huios), God has*
> *sent forth the Spirit of His Son into your hearts,*
> *crying out, "Abba, Father!" Therefore, you are no*
> *longer a slave but a son (huios), and if a son (huios),*
> *then an heir of God through Christ.* (Galatians
> 4:1–7 NKJV)

Being *born* of God means we have God's DNA implanted into our spirit. At this point, we are *"babes in Christ,"* and our journey has just begun. Unfortunately, far too many believers view this point as the climax—the end of the journey. They are *saved,* they are *redeemed,* they are God's *children*, they have their *ticket* punched, and now they only have to *sit back* and wait for that great express train to heaven.

That may be all that we want, but according to these Scriptures inspired by the Holy Spirit, that is not what God wants (*and after all, it is His plan, not ours, isn't it?*).

What does God want? Well, read the plan.

He desires "*sons*" (*huios*) to be "*joint*-heirs," with Christ, of the Kingdom of God. He wants His Son to have a bride—the *Ekklesia*—that is you and me, a bride "worthy" to receive the groom. As wonderful and marvelous as salvation is, it is not the end of the journey; it is but the beginning. Jesus did not die to "*redeem*" us so we could sit back on our haunches. He died so we would mature into a "*son of God*" worthy of hire, a son who has compassion for the lost and does all he can to bring them home!

> *The Spirit Himself bears witness with our spirit that we are children (teknon) of God, and if children (teknon), then heirs—heirs of God and joint-heirs (huios) with Christ, if indeed we suffer (maturity) with Him, that we may also be glorified together.* (Romans 8:16–17 NKJV)

When we acknowledge and accept Jesus as Lord and Savior, then we are "*born again*" *into the Kingdom* of God. As we mature and grow, under the tutorage of the Holy Spirit, we mature into the *huios* of God and become heirs and joint-heirs with Christ upon our *graduation*. Notice that maturing involves suffering with Him. What suffering?

> *Then Jesus said to His disciples, "If anyone desires to come after Me, let him deny himself, and take up his cross, and follow Me."* (Matthew 16:24 NKJV)

Our salvation was through the *Work of the Cross*. The maturing process is the *Life of the Cross*. The Holy Spirit now enters our spirits and begins the tutoring process. What *tutoring* process? Recall the Roman adoption was a two-step process. First was the *manci'patio,* the purchase of the person from one family into another family. The Father makes the sale and welcomes the person into his family.

Our Father completed the sale for us and paid for it with the blood of His Begotten Son. The past is erased, all debts are paid, and we become a greatly loved child (*teknon*) of God's family.

This is where so many stop, believing there is no more other than *being good, going to church once a week*, and waiting for *graduation*. But it is not over. It has only begun. There is much work to do—many souls to harvest.

The second step of the *adoption* process was the *vindi'catio,* the legal action taken to formalize and finalize the inheritance transfer process. This step was not automatic. For it to happen, it required the selected person's development into a mature, capable, participative member of the family. That *development'* period could be rough. There was correction involved, discipline issued, testing administered. *Maturity* carries a price tag. The Holy Spirit takes over and begins tutoring us through the Word, through revelation, and through the power of "Caught, not Taught."

<u>Jesus is coming for a spotless "bride"</u>

Paul used this Roman concept because it is precisely what happens to believers and is exactly what God intended before the "*foundations of the universe were laid.*" It is conceivable that the Holy Spirit inspired the Roman Empire into this adoption format just so it could be easily demonstrated and understood by believers down through time.

God's plan is to have a family of mature sons and daughters as coheirs with His Begotten Son, Jesus.

This was the intention of the Creator from the beginning—and it remains so to this day.

> *The mystery which has been hidden from ages and from generations, but now has been revealed to His saints.* (Colossians 1:26 NKJV)

How? Through the Word of God and through the indwelling power of the Holy Spirit. God will *save* us by having us being "*born again*" into His Holy *Family*, and then He would indwell inside of us to teach us, council us, test us, train us, equip us, intercede for us, guide us, warn us, baby us, and correct us!

Wow! What a plan! From the beginning, God wanted fellowship. He wanted to share His glory, to dwell and fellowship with His creation—His people—from the initial "*walking in the garden*" with Adam; to the detailed construction of the tabernacle in the wilderness of Sinai; to the magnificent temple of King Solomon; to the *Ekklesia*, the *church*, consisting of you and me and millions of others, from across time and from around the world, all united together as the corporate temple of God, the Body of Christ! He would fellowship in this "*temple*," the "*temple of the living God*," Jesus Christ as the Head, and we as the body. He formulated a *plan* and put it all in motion before He created any living or nonliving thing. All we must do is to say *yes* and allow the Holy Spirit to proceed "*transforming*" us into the "*body*," and we are a part of that eternal plan!

> *And not only this but also we ourselves, having the first fruits of the Spirit, even we ourselves groan within ourselves, waiting eagerly for our adoption as sons, the redemption of our body.* (Romans 8:23 NASB)

Did you catch that? Even the Apostle Paul was waiting for *graduation*—the final sealing of the *adoption* process—and he makes it clear that the final step will come with the "*redemption of our body*." Paul did not receive it while living on this earth!

The reward? How about an eternity of ruling and reigning alongside the King of kings? How about an eternity of sharing in the *glory* and *love* the Lord had with the Father?

That is what it is all about!

> *And now, O Father, glorify Me together with Yourself, with the glory which I had with You before*

the world was… And the glory which You gave Me
I have given them, that they may be one just as We
are one: I in them, and You in Me; that they may be
made perfect in one, and that the world may know
that You have sent Me, and have loved them as You
have loved Me. (John 17:5, 22–23 NKJV)

Did you also catch that? What Jesus said in the above prayer? *"You have loved them as You loved Me."* Wow! God loves us just as much as He loves His Begotten Son, Jesus! Again a double wow!

We should not look at this transformation from *child* to *son* as a progression. Advancing to *son* does not stop us from being *child*, a *child* of God whom He loves dearly! As a *born-again child* of God, He lavishes His love on us. He gives us life—and more abundantly! No, not the "things" of this temporal world but the things that the world doesn't have to give. Things like *true* joy, inner peace, heartfelt happiness and living, walking, and moving in the security of knowing that God, the Creator, is our Father. Those are beyond cost, beyond earthly value and worth, and which the world does not and cannot possess and, resultantly, cannot give or take away.

As we progress in our training and development into mature *sons*, God's love for us never changes. He cannot love us any more than He does, and His love never falters, pauses, or decreases. We will always be His *children*. We change—not God. We become more in the *"image of Christ"* and, as such, begin radiating those same *gifts* God gave to us into the world.

We had seen that from *before creation*, the Triune God looked down time and devised a plan whereby He would have a *Family* of mature sons to rule and reign as coheirs with His Begotten Son, Jesus. Our foundational Scripture of Ephesians 1:3–4 could be paraphrased as follows:

> *Before the Triune Godhead laid the first brick*
> *of the foundation of the world, or put a hammer to*
> *a nail… They had a board meeting and established*
> *the plan of how accepted (born again) children of*

God, would come into the Kingdom of God and transform into mature sons of God, in the image of the Son and through the tutoring of the Holy Spirit, as was the loving intention of the Father, so that they would coinherit the Kingdom with Jesus Christ.

That was God's intent before creation, during creation, and since creation to this day.

His intent and purpose have not changed.

Jesus is coming for His bride, a bride *without spot or wrinkle*, a bride that has prepared herself and is ready and able to meet her *bridegroom*. That bride will be found ready.

We are that bride.

That "getting ready" is the maturing process.

We need to get ready.

CHAPTER 11

TUTORING

Jesus was born a *brephos* (*an infant*). He matured; was baptized; went to the desert; fulfilled His ministry; went to the cross—fulfilled His destiny; rose from the tomb; and ascended to the Father as a *huios* (*the Begotten Son of God*).

Jesus was the "*first fruit,*" and His life established the methodology of God's plan: *be legally born into God's family and then mature under tutorage to sonship and inheritance.* Jesus was born a *child.* The Holy Spirit directed Him into becoming a mature *Son of God while being human.* His life was (is) the model for us to follow.

Jesus not only *established* the *Plan*; *He was and is the Plan*! Jesus is the "message." His life revolved around the cross and the Kingdom.

Our life's purpose is to be like Him in all ways.

God's Ultimate Plan

God's *Ultimate Intention, Purpose, and Plan* for creation have been revealed to us, and it follows the template Jesus presented. It too revolves around the cross and the Kingdom.

At some beautiful point in our life, the Holy Spirit stirs our spirits, and our souls awaken to Jesus as our personal Savior. We answer the call in the affirmative, accepting Jesus, and the Holy Spirit enters our spirit and we are "born again" as a *child citizen* of God's Kingdom.

But as many, as received Him (Jesus), to them
He gave the right to become children of God (teknon),
to those who believe in His name: who were born,
not of blood, nor of the will of the flesh, nor of the
will of man, but of God. (John 1:12–13 NKJV)

"It is finished." The price is *paid*; the work is *done!* There is nothing for us to do—no works, no rituals, no stations, no indulgences. *Jesus defeated all the enemies. HE rose from the tomb—from the embrace of death! The Son reigns in glory, seated at the right hand of the Father! All authority has been given to Him, all inheritance is His, all praise is His. And we, as FATHER's children, can enter into that glory with Him!*

Behold what manner of love the Father has
bestowed on us, that we should be called children of
God! (1 John 3:1 NKJV)

That was the intention of the FATHER. That is what the cross that Jesus willingly submitted Himself to—did for us. That is the WORK of the cross. But it does not stop at the WORK of the cross. The life, death, and resurrection of Jesus was the FATHER's purpose, but they are not the FATHER's *ULTIMATE* PURPOSE.

It all revolves around the cross and the Kingdom.

His death and resurrection was the *work* of the cross.

His life—the way He lived—is the *life* of the cross.

God desires more from us

Rebirth, salvation, redemption are *wonderful* and *marvelous* gifts, given to us *freely* from the FATHER, and they are a critical part of the plan, a part that puts us back on the road to His ULTIMATE INTENTION and PURPOSE with creation.

Jesus answered, "Truly, truly, I say to you,
unless one is born of water and the Spirit, he cannot
enter the kingdom of God." (John 3:5 NASB)

Being *born again as* a *"child of God"* opens the doors of heaven and gives us admittance into the Kingdom of God as legal citizens. But God's *Ultimate Purpose* for us is far more than only *"citizenship"* in the Kingdom.

Citizenship into the Kingdom of God is a *gift—freely given* by the FATHER. With that gift comes forgiveness and the total erasure of our former life. HE wipes the old "tapes" clean, and we start fully justified (*righteous*) in His eyes. When He looks at us, He sees Jesus wrapped around us. God sees no sin, no rebellion; He only sees His love for us.

And it is the *very beginning of our journey* with Christ into the FATHER'S ULTIMATE PURPOSE.

Being "born" of God means we have God's DNA implanted into our spirit, and we indeed are *"new babes"* in Christ. Far too many believers view this *as the climax—the end of their journey.* It is not the end; it is just the beginning. Instead of shouting what we are *saved from,* we should be shouting what we are *saved for! The Kingdom has come. Jesus brought it, and it resides inside of us now. We are saved to save the world—to take the Kingdom inside of us out into the world.*

Our journey has just begun.

> *Just as He chose us in Him before the foun-dation of the world, that we would be holy and blameless before Him. In love, He predestined us to adoption as sons through Jesus Christ to Himself, according to the kind intention of His will.* (Ephesians 1:4–6 NASB)

Some cannot get past the wonder of *salvation, redemption, for-giveness,* and *citizenship* in the Kingdom. These certainly are things to shout, dance, and rejoice in, but this is not the place to park in. We are *born again* into the Kingdom of God to *fulfill* God's purpose. The FATHER'S plan for His children is to become *"adopted as sons"* through Christ.

God does not desire for us to sit around the campfire. There is much work to do, a plentiful harvest to gather in, and He looks to His *"sons and daughters"* to be the harvesters.

> *Then He said to His disciples, "The harvest truly is plentiful, but the laborers are few. Therefore, pray to the Lord of the harvest that He will send out laborers into His harvest."* (Matthew 9:37–38 NKJV)

God desires a mature *family* of sons and daughters.

> *In Him also we have received an inheritance, being predestined (planned) according to the purpose of Him who works all things according to the counsel of His own will…to the praise of His glory.* (Ephesians 1:11–14, 17 MEV)

These Scriptures reveal God's *Ultimate Purpose*. Through God's Son, Jesus Christ, when we believe in Him and when we *"live for the praise of His glory,"* we will receive an inheritance according to *God's glory and plan.*

Notice that this plan came about as a *"council"* decision. What *"council"* would that be? A *council* is a meeting among members. This *"council"* meeting occurred *before* the *"foundations of the world were laid."* There can only have been one group of members to hold such a *council*, the TRIUNE GODHEAD—FATHER, SON, and HOLY SPIRIT! They met and put a *plan* together to share Their glory and Kingdom with Their creation, a creation that They had not yet created!

The Process

In the previous chapter, we unpacked the Greek word *huio'thesia* as understood within the Roman Empire as *"adopted as sons."* We saw that it meant the tutoring and maturing of a newly legal *member* of the family into a responsibility and inheritance position. The father established the tutor's plan to educate, train, develop, and discipline the new *member* from being a *child* into becoming a mature *son* worthy to carry on the father's name.

God established His *plan*, which includes all that is needed for us to mature into "*sons*" worthy of the "*inheritance*" to coreign with Jesus. That *plan* is centered around His begotten Son, Jesus the Messiah.

> *And now He alone is the leader and source of everything needed in the church. God has put every-thing beneath the authority of Jesus Christ and has given Him the highest rank above all others. And now we, His church, are His body on the earth, and that which fills Him, who is being filled by it!* (Ephesians1:22–23 TPT)

The PURPOSE of the PLAN is all about LOVE—the FATHER'S LOVE for His children.

The PROCESS of the PLAN is all about *tutoring* and *maturing* within the Kingdom.

After the WORK of the cross was *"finished," Jesus left*. He rejoined the FATHER and is seated at His right hand. He left us with these words:

> *Go* therefore and *make disciples of all nations, baptizing them in the name of the Father and of the Son and the Holy Spirit, teaching them to observe all things I have commanded you. And remember, I am with you always, even to the end of the age.* (Matthew 28:19–20 MEV)

Even though Jesus left to rejoin the FATHER, the *Gospel did not leave*. The Gospel of the Kingdom of GOD *remained on earth*, and *believers* are given the commission to *take it to all nations*. But here is the catch; babies cannot take anything anywhere, can they? To do so, we must mature from being children of God (*baby citizens of the Kingdom*) to sons of God (*inheritor citizens of the Kingdom*).

At this point, we begin our *walk with Christ*, and now, more than ever, our free will comes into play. There is a decision to be made, a decision carrying as much weight as our initial decision to accept Christ as our Lord or not. And here is where many stall in their "walk."

How far does one desire to "*walk*" with Christ? How close does one choose to "*live*" like Christ? Similar to our salvation, those questions *require individual decisions*, decisions that every believer in Jesus Christ makes, whether consciously or not. And they are not one-time decisions. It is a *decision process* that is made continually—day by day, hour by hour, minute by minute—at home, at the grocery store, at the barbershop, at the workplace, at school.

And here is the kicker. While the invitation to "legally" have "citizenship" in the family is *freely given and carries no price tag on our part*, these other, continuous, on-going decisions carry a price—a high price. Unfortunately, many do not wish to pay that price. *What is the cost?*

It is the total death of *self*.

> *Then Jesus said to His disciples, "If anyone desires to come after Me, let him deny himself, and take up his cross, and follow Me."* (Matthew 16:24 NKJV)

> *And do not be conformed to this world, but be transformed by the renewing of your mind, so that you may prove what the will of God is.* (Romans 12:2 NASB)

> *For those who live according to the flesh have their outlook shaped by the things of the flesh, but those who live according to the Spirit have their outlook shaped by the things of the Spirit.* (Romans 8:5 NKJV)

From the beginning, God desired fellowship—fellowship whereby He could share His GLORY with His creation! HE put in the *plan* to return to His original purpose—walking in the garden with Adam and Eve. God desired to once again *walk* in the garden *with* His creation. All Scripture, all history, the development of *a* chosen people, the Law, His Son taking human form and His resulting crucifixion and resurrection, His Gospel, and the infilling dwelling of the Holy Spirit all fit into God's *plan* for humankind to return to the garden.

> *Therefore repent and return, so that your sins may be wiped away, so that times of refreshing may come from the presence of the Lord; and that He may send Jesus, the Christ appointed for you, whom heaven must receive until the period of restoration of all things, about which God spoke by the mouths of His holy prophets from ancient times.* (Acts 3:19–21 NASB)

To fulfill this PLAN, a *dedicated effort* is required, dedicated by us, the body of Christ—dedication of our time, our talents, our commitment, our resources, our worldview and a dedicated commitment to *how we live every moment.*

As *"born again"* children in the Kingdom of God, we ask these questions: *What does maturing look like? How do I mature from a child of God to a son of God?* What is that process, and what is my *role* in it? How do I prepare myself for our Lord's return? How do I carry out the Great Commission?

Whereas *"justification"* is the first stage of the *adoption* process—*the legal purchase and inclusion of the individual into the family*—*"sanctification"* is the second stage of the process, *the maturing from child to son.*

Maturing

Our spirit comes from our Creator, *His breath*, a small touch of His DNA that stirs within us, seeking its source. Our spirits have the ability to reach out and interact within the spiritual realm. *We can detect and discern the voice of God when He calls to us.*

Our soul is caught in the middle of our spirit and our body. It identifies with the body and the world through emotions, thoughts, desires, ambitions, and also with the spirit reaching out, seeking its Creator.

If left as is, we have a problem; we cannot find God on our own. We get in our own way.

But the Holy Spirit responds to our spirit and opens the door for us to know Him and accept Him—through His Son. His plan is for His children to mature and be a part of the Body of Christ. For that to happen, the *human soul must be brought into submission to the Son. Self-centered* must give way to *God-centered.* Sin, rebellion, the world, all things contrary to God, must be replaced with Christ. The Holy Spirit must bring our emotions and will into submission. That is the LIFE OF THE CROSS and is the second step of the *adoption* process.

Easy?

No, not for a minute.

Satan—the world—and our flesh will all get in the way, resist, and challenge our spirit and soul to evict the Holy Spirit from dwelling in us. Evict the Holy Spirit from the *"temple,"* and nothing is remaining. We are given much instruction on how to work with the Holy Spirit in defeating these foes. Each of Paul's letters provide us with instruction, encouragement, and strength. The writer of Hebrews also added this instruction:

> *Endure your suffering as discipline; God is treating you as sons (huios). For what son is there that a father does not discipline? But if you do not experience discipline, something all sons have shared in, then you are illegitimate and are not sons. Besides, we have experienced discipline from our earthly fathers, and we respected them; shall we not submit ourselves all the more to the Father of spirits and receive life? For they disciplined us for a little while as seemed good to them, but he does so for our benefit, that we may share his holiness. Now all discipline seems painful at the time, not joyful. But later, it produces the fruit of peace and righteousness for those trained by it.* (Hebrews 12:7–12 NKJV)

It is a battle—no, it is a war, a war that we fight until the day we are caught up with Him and receive the "graduation diploma" of a glorified body. It is a difficult road and requires sacrifice and discipline. The mature sons of God will suffer the rejection of this world. It means going upstream against the tidal current of human, fleshly kingdoms determined to control the world outside of God's will. The world will view sons as being in rebellion against their worldview. They will be expelled and ostracized as a societal threat needing removal. Look at what Jesus told His disciples:

> *If the world hates you, you know that it hated Me before it hated you. If you were of the world, the world would love you as its own. But because you are not of the world, since I chose you out of the world, the world therefore hates you. Remember the word that I said to you: "A servant is not greater than his master." If they persecuted Me, they will also persecute you. If they kept My words, they will keep yours also. But all these things they will do to you for My name's sake because they do not know Him who sent Me. He who hates me hates my Father also.* (John 15:18–22 MEV)

Left on our own, this is an impossible task. None of us could ever work hard enough to achieve the slightest headway in such an overpowering task. To overcome the world—overcome everything our senses see, hear, touch, smell, and feel—is *beyond human ability*.

To step out of *me* and not feel, think, or exist as *me is impossible to do on my own.*

The Tutor

Our God does not leave us alone to figure it out and do it on our own. He knows *we cannot.* He does not give us a commission we cannot fulfill. *HE equips us, HE empowers us,* and *HE provides us with a tutor,* a tutor no enemy or foe can resist or stand up against!

But the Helper, the Holy Spirit, whom the Father will send in My name, He will teach you all things, and bring to your remembrance all that I said to you. (John 14:26 NKJV)

Now we have not received the spirit of the world, but the Spirit who is from God, so that we may know the things that are freely given to us by God. (1 Corinthians 2:12 NKJV)

Moreover if the Spirit of the one who raised Jesus from the dead lives in you, the one who raised Christ from the dead will also make your mortal bodies alive through his Spirit who lives in you. (Romans 8:11 NASB)

He will indwell inside of us and EMPOWER us into becoming mature sons of God in Jesus Christ! Now somebody should be shouting!

This maturing from children to "sonship inheritance" is Holy Spirit discipline and teaching that will lead us into *disciplined holiness lives* until HE returns. This is Caught more than Taught.

FATHER, in His love and all-knowing wisdom, has not left us to fail. He has provided *a tutor,* one to walk with us, beside us, behind us, in front of us, and to live INSIDE of us so that He can deal directly with our flesh and our soul. Through the Word of God and the *indwelling power* of the Holy Spirit, *resulting in the death of our fleshly man,* the Gospel goes forth into all the world as Jesus commanded.

What is the enemy's number one weapon he continually attempts to wield in his war to halt the spread of the Gospel of the Kingdom? It is the hijacking of the Holy Spirit from having any power or relevance in the Christian walk. Remove the car's fuel, and no matter how beautiful the car looks or how many bells and whistles it has, the car goes nowhere. It sits there like a monolith, a beautiful idol with no power, no relevance, and does nothing. How many beautiful architectural structures stand across the globe, proclaiming to be the dwelling places of God Almighty that are nothing but lifeless, powerless temples of stone and wood?

The *Holy Spirit is the fuel—the power—*that *transforms* us from being fleshly into *powerful beacons of light* blaring out into the darkness of a world of kingdoms that deny its Creator and Savior. Sadly, over the generations and across the globe, the enemy has been phenomenally successful in his goal of dismissing the HOLY SPIRIT and putting HIM on the back burner. But the Holy Spirit has always had a "*remnant*" that stood up for the Gospel and the Kingdom.

Jesus did nothing without the Holy Spirit. When Jesus was baptized in the Jordan River, the Holy Spirit descended on Him:

> *And when Jesus was baptized, He came up immediately out of the water. And suddenly the heavens were opened to Him, and He saw the Spirit of God descending on Him like a dove. And a voice came from heaven, saying, "This is My beloved Son, in whom I am well pleased." (Matthew 3:16–17 MEV)*

It was at that point that His ministry began.

Following His resurrection, Jesus spent considerable time with His disciples, and upon leaving, He did not send them out but told them to wait in Jerusalem for the *"Another"* to come who would give them all that they would need to take the Gospel into the world.

> *But you shall receive power when the Holy Spirit comes upon you. And you shall be My witnesses in Jerusalem, and all Judea and Samaria, and to the ends of the earth. (Acts 1:8 MEV)*

And the "Another" came:

> *Suddenly a sound like a mighty rushing wind came from heaven, and it filled the whole house where they were sitting. There appeared to them*

tongues as of fire, being distributed and resting on
each of them, and they were all filled with the Holy
Spirit. (Acts 2:2–4 MEV)

With this power, these common men turned a sinful, rebellious, anti-God world upside down and established the Kingdom of God on earth amidst a world full of godless kingdoms!

Diamonds in the Rough

When we come to Christ as our Lord and Savior, we are like dirty, rough, discolored diamonds, diamonds just dug out of the dirt and mud, hard, unfinished stones, stained and discolored.

Accepting Jesus Christ as Lord and Savior, we become "*children of God*" with entrance into the kingdom of God. On that glorious day, *salvation* "cleans" the dirt away so that God only sees the diamond underneath. God is light, and as He cleans with the blood of the Lamb, His light begins penetrating into us and reflecting back out into the world. It may be a dim light; it may be a slightly reddish light due to the blood of the lamb, *but for the first time in our existence, we transmit God's light into the dark world.*

When we *decide to truly turn our life over to Christ and live for Him*, the Master Jeweler—the Holy Spirit—moves into our spirit and takes up residence. He scrapes and cleans the remaining dirt and discolor away from the diamond and then begins cutting. He knows exactly what cuts to make for each individual diamond to bring out the brightest, sparkling reflection of God's light. He knows where to start and how deep to make them. Once HE finishes a cut, HE polishes the surface into a high, pure, supernatural reflective gloss. He does not pause in HIS work, and as soon as one facet is complete, HE immediately begins working on the next facet. Jesus is the perfect diamond—*the Holy Spirit works to make us more into the image of Jesus.*

What cuts does HE make? What does HE remove?

Adultery, sexual immorality, impurity, lewdness, idolatry, sorcery, hatred, strife, jealousy, rage,

134

selfishness, dissensions, heresies, envy, murders, drunkenness, carousing, and the like. I warn you, as I previously warned you, that those who do such things shall not inherit the kingdom of God. (Galatians 5:19–21 MEV paraphrased)

HE removes all the worldly garbage and then polishes the facets with the "fruit" of the *Spirit*:

But the fruit of the Spirit is love, joy, peace, patience, gentleness, goodness, faith, meekness, and self-control; against such, there is no law. Those who are Christ's have crucified the flesh with its passions and lusts. If we live in the Spirit, let us also walk in the Spirit. (Galatians 5:22–25 MEV)

But as He who has called you is holy, so be holy in all your conduct, because it is written, "Be holy, for I am holy." (1 Peter 1:15–16 MEV)

What emerges is a multifaceted, sparkling diamond that receives the "light" from the FATHER and retransmits it into a dark, lightless world. The mature sons and daughters of GOD ARE the "light (the sparkle) of the world."

You are the light of the world. A city (diamond) set on a hill cannot be hidden. (Matthew 5:14 NASB)

Who will transform the body of our humble state into conformity with the body of His glory, by the exertion of the power that He has even to subject all things to Himself. (Philippians 3:20–21 NASB)

Uncut, each diamond is only a hard stone. It is still a diamond, but it reflects no light, holds no "sparkle," and adds nothing to the

Kingdom. Each one must be cut perfectly to match each stone's material, shape, and quality. The Holy Spirit performs the most exquisite cuts across the entire surface of the diamond, cuts that are designed to allow the maximum light to reflect outward into the world. The majority of these "cuts" are lessons Caught, not Taught.

> *For you were formerly darkness, but now you*
> *are light in the Lord. Walk as children of light.*
> (Ephesians 5:8 NASB)

It is a process that continues throughout our entire earthly life. God is light. As each painful cut is made, more of the FATHER's "*light*" shines forth into the dark world. The closer we draw to God, the more of HIS light we reflect into the world.

> *Move your heart closer and closer to God, and*
> *he will come even closer to you.* (James 4:8 TPT)

Conversely, the further we draw away from God, the less "light" we "reflect" into the world. The closer we draw to the world, the less light we shine forthwith, therefore,

> *and do not have fellowship with the unfruit-*
> *ful works of darkness; instead, expose them. For it is*
> *shameful even to speak of those things which are done*
> *by them in secret. But all things are exposed when*
> *they are revealed by the light, for everything that*
> *becomes visible is light.* (Ephesians 5:11–13 MEV)

Continuing to draw away, we ultimately reflect no light and become only a darkened, hidden stone for someone to stumble over. How many people have "stumbled" over "darkened Christians," Christians who think they are diamonds but, in reality, are only stumbling stones?

Adam was made and molded by God Himself as a perfectly cut diamond—a child of the "light." When Adam chose to eat of the Tree of Knowledge, he was telling God he did not need or want God's cuts but that he could make his own cuts. Of course, what he ended up with was a defective diamond that only reflected fractured, impure light, and with God now more distant from him, there was less light to reflect. Unfortunately, we have followed in Adam's footsteps.

The process of maturing is the death of *self* and the transformation of our souls through the renewing of our minds into the image of Christ. It is a lifelong process that never ends until graduation. The Holy Spirit always finds one more cut to make.

The Cross

We are warned of the pitfalls and given much instruction on working with the Holy Spirit in defeating our three foes—our carnal flesh, the world, and satan. Paul's Letters provide us with instruction, encouragement, and strength.

> *Walk holy, in a way that is suitable to your high rank, given to you in your divine calling. With tender humility and quiet patience, always demonstrate gentleness and generous love toward one another... Be faithful to guard the sweet harmony of the Holy Spirit among you in the bonds of peace, being one body and one spirit, as you were all called into the same glorious hope of divine destiny. For the Lord God is one, and so are we, for we share in one faith, one baptism, and one Father. And He is the perfect Father who leads us all, works through us all, and lives in us all. (Ephesians 4:1–6 TPT)*

This is the LIFE OF THE CROSS; this is what Paul meant when He said,

> *For if we have been united with Him in the likeness of His death, so shall we also be united with Him in the likeness of His resurrection, knowing this, that our old man has been crucified with Him,*

so that the body of sin might be destroyed, and we should no longer be slaves to sin... Likewise, you also consider yourselves to be dead to sin but alive to God through Jesus Christ our Lord. Therefore, do not let sin reign in your mortal body, that you should obey it in its lusts. Do not yield your members to sin as instruments of unrighteousness, but yield yourselves to God, as those who are alive from the dead, and your bodies to God as instruments of righteousness. For sin shall not have dominion over you, for you are not under the law, but under grace. (Romans 6:5–14 MEV)

This is the "maturing" process, the total death of "self" and living a life in this present world dedicated to following and obeying the *tutor*—the Holy Spirit.

It is our opinion that while there are millions of believers who will partake of the Kingdom, there is a smaller number—a remnant, Scripture calls them—down through the ages, who have progressed from *child to son*, qualifying to rule and reign with Him. *To do so requires a daily dying to the world and to yourself, placing Christ above yourself in all things, at all times, following and obeying the Holy Spirit in every aspect of one's life.* This is sanctification and begins the minute we acknowledge and accept Jesus as our Lord and does not end until "graduation" (the Lord's return).

How do I know how I am doing?

We ask ourselves, how do I know if I'm moving forward in the maturing process?

That is a fair question, one that no other person is qualified or capable of answering. Only God knows what is in the *heart* of man.

The answer we offer is one word: Prayer.

No—we do not mean *"Now I lay me down to sleep."* That is not prayer; that is recital.

We mean a real prayer life. And that does not mean spending hours wearing out the knees of your trousers either. It means having ongoing working communication with the FATHER.

Keep in mind what *prayer* is. It is talking with the FATHER. Think about that. *With* is the keyword. It is not us always telling God what we need, want, desire, or wish for. It is not us just crying and feeling sorry for ourselves to God. It is not us dominating the conversation. Prayer is simply a word for "talking with God." This means it is listening as well as speaking. God will talk to you, if you give Him a chance to get a word in edgewise.

> *Be still and know that I am God; I will be exalted among the nations; I will be exalted in the earth!* (Psalm 46:10 NKJV)

Our goal is to become more like the image of Christ and to be Holy as God is Holy. Who is best to tell you how you are doing at that than the FATHER? We propose no one else could even attempt to. Only God knows your motivations. He knows where you are regarding holiness. He knows where you are in fulfilling your calling. He knows where you are regarding humility, compassion, caring, kindness, meekness, patience, unity, peace and how well you are doing at putting off the old man and putting on the new man. The Holy Spirit dwells inside of us, and He knows what he has asked us to do and what has been done regarding it to include the attitude behind your doing it. It is not all about *what* you do but more so *why* you do it that God looks at. All those things are a measurement of *"How am I doing?"*

Prayer is communication—two-way communication. Prayer is talking to Father no different than talking to your family. Ask God how you are doing. Trust me; He will tell you. You just need to keep quiet for a bit and let Him speak to you. You will know. In fact, one measurement of "How am I doing?" is "How is your prayer life?" If it is good, then you are doing good! If it is not, then you know you need to work on it and probably some other things as well.

Look at it this way: you would not live with your family and only talk to them for ten minutes each morning telling them what you wanted for that day and then not speak to them again for the rest of the day (at least we hope you would not). God is no different, yet that is exactly what millions of "Christians" do each day. He is your FATHER, the best FATHER you have, and HE enjoys talking with you all day. Develop that relationship, and HE will let you know, without any question or ambiguity, exactly *how you are doing.*

The measurement for maturity is measured against one fundamental parameter: *how well are you putting what Christ wants from you first and putting what you want last?* Do not rationalize and do not listen to yourself. Open your heart to hear God's heart, and He will tell you.

Our maturity is not measured by the size or type of "mission" God has for us but by how we respond to it.

When our souls are in sync and in agreement with our spirit, we have been TRANSFORMED. *We have matured—we have gained an inheritance in the Kingdom to rule and reign with the King.*

The Apostle Paul said,

> *And those who are Christ's have crucified the flesh with its passions and desires.* (Galatians 5:24 NKJV)

> *But may I never boast except in the cross of our Lord Jesus Christ, through which the world has been crucified to me, and I to the world.* (Galatians 6:14 NASB)

> *We know that our old man was crucified with him so that the body of sin would no longer dominate us so that we would no longer be enslaved to sin.* (Romans 6:6 NKJV)

> *I have been crucified with Christ, and it is no longer I who live, but Christ lives in me. So, the life*

I now live in the body, I live because of the faith-
fulness of the Son of God, who loved me and gave
himself for me. (Galatians 2:20 MEV)

And do not present your members to sin as
instruments to be used for unrighteousness but pres-
ent yourselves to God as those who are alive from the
dead and your members to God as instruments to be
used for righteousness. (Romans 6:13 NKJV)

Therefore, I exhort you, brothers and sisters,
by the mercies of God, to present your bodies as a
sacrifice—alive, holy, and pleasing to God—which
is your reasonable service. (Romans 12:1 MEV)

These are the sons of God:

The eager expectation of the creation waits for
the appearance of the sons of God. For the creation
was subjected to futility, not willingly, but by the
will of Him who subjected it, in hope that the cre-
ation itself also will be set free from its slavery to
corruption into the glorious freedom of the children
of God. We know that the whole creation groans
and travails in pain together until now. (Romans
8:20–22 TPT)

We must always keep in mind that this second phase of our journey with Christ is not about salvation; it is about carrying out His Great
Commission and being the Ambassadors of Light in a dark world. The
"works" we do, coupled with the motivation of why we are doing them,
following our salvation determines our inheritance and reward.

Jesus said,

Do not store up for yourselves treasures on
earth where moth and rust destroy and where

thieves break in and steal. But store up for your-
selves treasures in heaven, where neither moth nor
rust destroy and where thieves do not break in nor
steal, for where your treasure is, there will your heart
be also. (Matthew 6:19–21 MEV)

Be sure that you not do your charitable deeds
before men to be seen by them. Otherwise you have
no reward from your Father who is in heaven.
Therefore, when you do your charitable deeds, do
not sound a trumpet before you as the hypocrites do
in the synagogues and in the streets, that they may be
honored by men. Truly I say to you, they have their
reward. But when you do your charitable deeds, do
not let your left hand know what your right hand is
doing, that your charitable deeds may be in secret.
And your Father who sees in secret will Himself
reward you openly. (Matthew 6:1–4 MEV)

For just as the body without the spirit is dead,
so also faith without works is dead. (James 2:26
MEV)

Jesus closed the *Diary* with the following:

Look, I am coming soon! My reward is with
Me to give to each one according to his work.
(Revelation 22:12 MEV)

"What he has done"—done for what? For his salvation?

No, it is not what he has done *"for"* salvation; it is what he has
done WITH salvation.

As we progress in our training and development, God's love for
us never changes. He cannot love us any more than He does, and
His love never falters, pauses, or decreases. We will always be His
children.

And He chose us to be His very own, joining us to Himself even before He laid the foundation of the universe. Because of His great love, He ordained us, so that we would be holy in His eyes with an unstained innocence. For it was always in His perfect plan to adopt us as His delightful children, through our union with Jesus, the Anointed One, so that His tremendous love that cascades over us would glorify His grace—for the same love He has for His Beloved One, Jesus, He has for us. And this unfolding plan brings Him great pleasure. (Ephesians 1:4–6 TPT)

Our journey continues. We have a commission from our King—to be empowered by the Holy Spirit and to take the Gospel into all the world so that one day, soon, we will share in the Kingdom of God.

That is our FATHER'S ULTIMATE INTENTION, PURPOSE, and PLAN. Sitting back, waiting for the Lord's return is not.

Yes, we can do such if we wish to, but what joy and gladness do we miss by not becoming part of the "prepared" Bride of our Lord, Savior, and King and to share with Him the joys of the Kingdom of the Father?

What JOY is missed when we are not in "HIS GLORY"?

I pray with great faith for you because I'm fully convinced that the One who began this glorious work in you will faithfully continue the process of maturing you and will put his finishing touches to it until the unveiling of our Lord Jesus Christ! (Philippians 1:6 TPT)

CHAPTER 12

"THY KINGDOM COME"

What a journey we have been on! We have seen that the Creator of all things did so with a *Purpose and Plan*. It is God's *Purpose and Plan* for His children to be *redeemed* from their disobedience and sin and to turn back to Him and then move on into *maturity as co-inheritors of the Kingdom*. God's *Ultimate Intention, Purpose, and Plan* revolves around not only being citizens of the kingdom of God but being a family of sons and daughters for all eternity with FATHERLOVE.

Knowing this now leaves us with the question: *What exactly is the Kingdom of God?*

Well, we know where to find that answer now, don't we? It is back to the *Diary*—the Holy Scriptures.

As we have seen, no single book of the Holy Scriptures is dedicated to revealing God's *Ultimate Intention, Purpose, and Plan* with creation, but when taken as a whole, it reveals it from cover to cover! The entire Bible is the story of God's Plan for achieving His *Purpose*. From the opening pages in Genesis in the garden to the new heavens and earth in Revelation, God reveals His plan to expand His glory and love throughout His Kingdom.

The Greek word used for *kingdom*[16] is *basileia*, and from a theological view, it means:

> *The rule of God within the Realm in which*
> *He rules.*

Realm in this sense means *a territory, a land; a people; both natural and spiritual.*

Rule and realm are key words when defining the Kingdom.

We Begin at the Beginning

To understand the *Kingdom of God*, the place to begin is at the "*beginning.*"

> *In the beginning, God created the heaven and*
> *the earth.* (Genesis 1:1 NASB)

This simple opening verse of the *Diary* captures the totality of the *realm* and the *rule* of the Kingdom.

The *realm* consists of everything—before and after creation. Before anything else existed, God was; therefore, everything is in the *realm* of God's Kingdom.

The *rule* is El Shaddai—God Almighty, God All-Powerful, All-Knowledgeable, All-Magnificent. He created all things; therefore, He rules over all things. He...alone...is KING.

> *All things came into being through Him, and*
> *apart from Him not even one thing came into being*
> *that has come into being.* (John 1:3 NASB)

His manifest glory is the sharing of His *realm* and *rule* with His creation—all the beauty and mystery to expand it and share it with us.

---

[16] *Strong's Expanded Exhaustive Concordance of the Bible*, 2010, 51.

The visible felt glory of God is the manifest presence of His LOVE.

He existed before anything. He has more power and authority than anything. God is sovereign. He created *all* things. There is none greater or equal to God. Therefore, the logic is simple and straightforward—*the Kingdom of God is everything*. He alone is King over all things, material and spiritual. *Therefore, all things, temporal and spiritual, are encompassed in His Kingdom.*

From *before the foundations of the world were laid*, it was in God's heart to create a *dwelling* place for Himself where He could *expand* His glory and love through His "*sons and daughters*" as "*coheirs*" of the kingdom through Jesus Christ.

Galaxies, solar systems, stars, planets, even space itself—all created by God, all full of His glory, His love, His power. As citizens of His Kingdom, honor His name in their magnificence and mystery. Every leaf of every tree is a "citizen" of His Kingdom. Life, with its microscopic support systems, each dependent upon the others for survival, pulses and thrives as a citizen in His Kingdom. When a sparrow falls, He knows. When the storm rages, He Knows. The all-powerful, all-knowing, all-loving FATHERLOVE watches over His Kingdom. He creates all things, through Him and for Him; therefore, all things are His Kingdom.

And His *Ultimate Intention and Plan* is to turn that over to us! Under the headship of Jesus Christ, this marvelous Kingdom is designed to be shared, expanded, and spread throughout the universe.

That was the original design of the *Garden of Eden* where all was in harmony with God's heart. That design got sidetracked by Adam and Eve's decision to turn away from God and choose their own path. Disharmony set in as sin (disobedience to God) encompassed all of creation. God's oversight of His Kingdom was voluntarily put aside. Everything of man's original dominion came under a curse as the relationship with the Father was fractured. Adam *forfeited his rule* over the earth and handed it over, lock, stock, and barrel, to satan.

And it did not take long until satan's rule over the earth and man's depravity resulted in God having to "step in" and remove all resultant stains of an abomination against His Creation with a worldwide *deluge*, sparing only a single *righteous* family.

Following the *deluge*, a *renewed order was established* by God for His Kingdom on earth. God decreed man to be *"fruitful and multiply,"* and he was again given dominion over all living things:

> *Then God blessed Noah and his sons and said to them, "Be fruitful and multiply and fill the earth. The fear of you and the terror of you will be on every animal of the earth and on every bird of the sky; on everything that crawls on the ground, and on all the fish of the sea. They are handed over to you."* (Genesis 9:1–3 NASB)

But this time, *man's relationship with his Creator was not as it was in the beginning.* The *deluge* did not restore the damaged relationship, nor did it eradicate satan's influence on creation and humankind, and it did not remove man's capacity for rebellion against God. Man is still fallen, but through the *grace* of God, there is hope for recovery of what was lost.

FATHERLOVE gave man a covenant:

> *Now behold, I Myself am establishing My covenant with you, and with your descendants after you... God said, "This is the sign of the covenant which I am making between Me and you and every living creature that is with you, for all future generations; I have set My rainbow in the cloud, and it shall serve as a sign of a covenant between Me and the earth."* (Genesis 9:9, 12–13 NASB)

God is the sovereign King of His Kingdom. His Kingdom dominates and permits all and every other kingdom, whether worldly or spiritual. His kingship transcends all ages, all nations, all governments, all time, and all happenings. It has no boundaries, whether in spiritual or material measures, and He holds all authority over all things. God is in *charge*.

But He handed *control* to Adam, who then handed it over to satan. As a result, man has lived a cursed existence, and God's Kingdom, created for His glory and expansion, has been under the curse of satan for the past six thousand or so years.

Today's world does not reflect the Kingdom of God as created or intended by the Father.

> *The entire universe is standing on tiptoe, yearning to see the unveiling of God's glorious sons and daughters! For against its will, the universe itself has had to endure the empty futility resulting from the consequences of human sin. But now, with eager expectation, all creation longs for freedom from its slavery to decay and to experience with us the wonderful freedom coming to God's children. To this day, we are aware of the universal agony and groaning of creation, as if it were in the contractions of labor for childbirth.* (Romans 8:19–22 TPT)

God's Plan for Renewal Commences

God's *Plan* unfolded across the pages of history. Choosing a *people* with whom to implement His plan, He prepared the world for the advent of His Son—and redemption. For two thousand years, He instructed, foretold, and educated the world of the most significant event coming in all of history.

Until, following four hundred years of silence, a *"voice in the wilderness"* came declaring,

> *Repent, for the kingdom of heaven is at hand.*
> (Matthew 3:2 NKJV)

Declaring the kingdom *was* "*at hand*," John the Baptizer announced that the true ruler of God's Kingdom was arriving, and HE was bringing the end to the power and rule of all evil—satan and human.

The kingdom was near because Jesus was near. The King would arrive, and His arrival, His presence, meant a new world order and hope for creation would arrive, along with the power of God. Man would no longer be held hostage to sin but could rise above the kingdoms of the world—satan's and of men—and through the power of the Holy Spirit, could confront satan and begin to overthrow his dominion over deprivation, disease, destruction, and death. Through Jesus, the blessings of God's Kingdom are available to humankind—now—to bring life and light to a world of death and darkness.

John's decree was followed by the Son of God, Jesus of Nazareth, declaring:

> *From that time Jesus began to preach and say,*
> *"Repent, for the kingdom of heaven is at hand."*
> (Matthew 4:17)

Stating that the "*Kingdom was at hand*," Jesus was proclaiming that the Kingdom was available—NOW! The prophets had said, "*He is coming*." Jesus was saying, "*He is here—I am HE*."

Sons and daughters did not have to wait for the Kingdom to arrive; it was here, all around them, and had arrived in the form of Jesus of Nazareth—the incarnate Son of God. The King has come, and believers can now live under His reign as King in the Kingdom—now—not having to wait until they leave their *earth suits* and go into God's presence. Jesus has been given all authority over heaven and earth to reign, and He reigns—now.

Jesus did not preach the *Gospel of Salvation*; He preached the *Gospel of the Kingdom*.

> *Now after John had been taken into custody,*
> *Jesus came into Galilee, preaching the gospel of God,*
> *and saying, "The time is fulfilled, and the kingdom*
> *of God is at hand; repent and believe in the gospel."*
> (Mark 1:14–15 NASB)

There is a distinctive difference between the Gospel of Salvation and the Gospel of the Kingdom. The Gospel of Salvation focuses on the death of Jesus on the cross. It is the blessed gift of FATHERLOVE to us and becomes the *foundation for our return* to His *Ultimate Purpose.* The *Gospel of Salvation stops at the empty tomb.*

The *Gospel of the Kingdom expands on this foundation* to include His resurrection, ascension, and enthronement. Both Gospels are required for God's purpose and plan to be carried out, and together they constitute the essence and heart of God.

The message of the Kingdom is *repentance* and *return to the garden.* Repentance is renunciation and reversal of life's course from *self-centered* to *God-centered.* It requires total submission of self to God for continual teachability and growth ability from *child* to *son.*

> But when the Spirit of truth comes, He will guide you into all truth, for He will not speak on His own authority. But He will speak whatever He hears, and He will tell you things that are to come. (John 16:13 NKJV)

> The Spirit Himself bears witness with our spirit that we are children of God, and if children, then heirs—heirs of God and joint-heirs with Christ, if indeed we suffer with Him, that we may also be glorified together. (Romans 8:16–17 NKJV)

Transformation is now available to occur within our spirits and souls. The Holy Spirit can enter and begin the tutoring process.

> For as many as are led by the Spirit of God, these are sons of God. (Romans 8:14 NKJV)

> Predestined to be conformed to the image of His Son. (Romans 8:29 NKJV)

Answering the call and coming to God in a spirit of obedience and humility opens the way for us to focus on helping others to be reconciled to God. This is advancing the Kingdom, and this is our assignment until Christ returns. *There is no growth in the Kingdom without obedience to the Holy Spirit.* Advancing the Kingdom of God on earth during our lifetime results in the production of fruit.

> *But others fell on good ground and yielded a*
> *crop: some a hundredfold, some sixty, some thirty.*
> (Matthew 13:8 NKJV)

Three Phases of the Kingdom

Jesus taught many things about the Kingdom using parables. Of the forty parables that Jesus taught in the Gospels, nineteen are direct references to the Kingdom. Through teaching like this, Jesus shows us the Kingdom status presently and in the future. The message of the Kingdom encompasses three different time eras—the present (Earth Age), the future (Kingdom Age), and eternity (Eternal Age).

First, the present, the Earth Age.

In this era, which is defined as every individual's lifespan, we are given the opportunity to recover our lost relationship with God and begin to recover our lost authority and rulership. The KING has come to begin this restoration! The Kingdom is being realized, one by one, as people come to accept the King in personal ways as their Lord and Savior.

Second, the future—the Kingdom Age

Jesus returns to the earth, this time not as a baby in a manger but as Lord and King on a white horse, with fire and sword. He comes to rule over all the kingdoms of the earth, and His *sons and daughters* reign and rule as coheirs in the millennium.

The Kingdom of God on earth will be fully established and conclusive upon the return of Jesus to earth. The prophet Daniel prophesized this event hundreds of years before Christ walked the earth:

> *And in the days of those kings the God of*
> *heaven will set up a kingdom which will never be*
> *destroyed, and that kingdom will not be left for*
> *another people; it will crush and put an end to all*

these kingdoms, but it will itself endure forever. Just as you saw that a stone was broken off from the mountain without hands, and that it crushed the iron, the bronze, the clay, the silver, and the gold. (Daniel 2:44–45)

The Kingdom of God will become a great mountain that will fill the entire earth:

Then the iron, the clay, the bronze, the silver, and the gold were crushed to pieces all at the same time, and they were like chaff from the summer threshing floors, and the wind carried them away so that not a trace of them was found. But the stone that struck the statue became a great mountain and filled the entire earth. (Daniel 2:35 NKJV)

And he who falls on this stone will be broken to pieces; but on whomever it falls, it will scatter him like dust. (Matthew 21:44 NKJV)

In this statement, Jesus is presenting the Kingdom in two stages—the present age and the Kingdom Age. The present age is defined as the time Jesus came to earth the first time until He returns the second time. He is the *"stone,"* and the Kingdom lives within Him. When we accept Jesus as our Savior, Lord, and King, we *"fall on this stone"* and are *"broken in pieces."* The Kingdom lives within us, and our commission is to share and spread the Kingdom wherever we are.

The second stage occurs upon the second coming of Jesus to earth when the *stone falls* on the kingdoms and peoples of the world and *"will scatter him like dust."* No man or kingdom will stand in opposition, but the Kingdom of God will forcefully regain the world.

For as in Adam all die, so also in Christ all will be made alive. But each in his own order: Christ the first fruits, after that those who are Christ's at His coming, then comes the end, when He hands over the kingdom to our God and Father when He has abolished all rule and all authority and power. For He must reign until He has put all His enemies under His feet. (1 Corinthians 15:22–25 NKJV)

Then the seventh angel sounded; and there were loud voices in heaven, saying, "The kingdom of the world has become the kingdom of our Lord and of His Christ; and He will reign forever and ever." (Revelation 11:15 NKJV)

The King has arrived! And so we begin the transformation from living under the kingdoms of the earth to living under the Kingdom of God—on earth.

For a child will be born to us, a son will be given to us, And the government will rest on His shoulders; And His name will be called Wonderful Counselor, Mighty God, Eternal Father, Prince of Peace. There will be no end to the increase of His government or of peace, On the throne of David and over his kingdom, To establish it and to uphold it with justice and righteousness From then on and forevermore. (Isaiah 9:6–7 NASB)

He shall judge between the nations, And rebuke many people; They shall beat their swords into plowshares, And their spears into pruning hooks; Nation shall not lift up sword against nation, Neither shall they learn war anymore. (Isaiah 2:4 NKJV)

Think of it, the glory of heaven touching earth.

God's plan from the beginning with the garden was to have His glory not only touch the earth but to thrive and expand on earth.

Adam created a detour, which required a significant course correction to get back on the right path.

God reigns in people who have traded their *self-centeredness* for *God-centeredness*, people who have willingly yielded to His gift of *love* and have formed a relationship with Him. That is how God's economy works: the rule of LOVE residing within the reign of LOVE.

This age of the Kingdom—the Millennium—next to the cross, is the greatest expression of FATHERLOVE! It is a time when God continues to give His love to those who have still not accepted His plan of salvation, a final time of extending the Kingdom to all the nations of the earth.

Third, eternity—the Eternal Age.

We will live, reign, and serve with the Triune Godhead for all eternity.

We must understand that *eternal life* consists of life not regulated or controlled by a timeline but instead is life swelling in the presence of the Triune Godhead. It is spiritual and overflows with inner peace, joy, goodness, and love, having no beginning and no end. Eternity cannot be measured or comprehended with any earthly or human measurements.

This era actually begins the moment we accept Jesus as Lord and Master; we enter into His eternal Kingship and reign. At some point, we exchange our *earth suits* for *glorified* bodies and continue on into eternity with our King.

So then God is reigning and ruling over His Kingdom realm Now and FOREVER! The kingdom is *life* eternal, a perspective of a victorious mindset that lives in the *now* and the *forever* simultaneously.

> *Your kingdom come. Your will be done, On*
> *earth as it is in heaven.* (Matthew 6:10 NASB)

Kingdom of heaven versus Kingdom of God

Sometimes these two terms confuse people, but it is evident from Scripture that these two terms are interchangeable. The text and numerous references in the Gospels make it clear that they are the same.

The term kingdom of God does not occur in the Old Testament. But the idea that God was supreme over all creation was clearly understood and stated.

> How awesome is the LORD Most High, the great King over all the earth! (Psalm 47:2 NIV)

> The LORD has established His throne in heaven, And His kingdom rules overall. (Psalm 103:19 NKJV)

> Your kingdom is an everlasting kingdom, And Your dominion endures throughout all generations. (Psalm 145:13 NASB)

The New Testament records over 154 references to "*the Kingdom*." Of these, 108 are attributed to Jesus's ministry, which was His entire theme and message.

The New Testament writers use the phrase "*the Kingdom of God*" a total of seventy-seven times. Matthew uses the term five times, while Mark uses it fourteen times; Luke, thirty-two times, and John, two times. It is recorded in the Book of Acts six times, and the Apostle Paul used it eight times in his writings. It is found once in the Book of Revelation.

Matthew refers to *Kingdom* fifty-three times in his short Gospel, five times as the *Kingdom of God* and thirty-four times as the *Kingdom of heaven,* four times as the *Father's Kingdom* and twice as the *Kingdom of the Son of Man.* The remaining eight are references to simply *Kingdom* having worldly designations.

Matthew is the only NT writer who uses the term "*Kingdom of heaven.*" Everyone else uses the "*Kingdom of God.*" There are two reasons for this:

First, Matthew's Gospel was written for his audience consisting predominately of the Jewish establishment. They would not speak (much less write) the name of God, so Matthew was showing his respect and reference for that.

Second, the other writers wrote mainly for Roman audiences, who could digest the *Kingdom of God* concept but not a *Kingdom of heaven* brought to earth. Their pagan gods had "kingdoms," but they were remote and apart from humans. It was a foreign concept to think of Olympia—home of the gods—coming to earth.

Characteristics of the Kingdom of God

The Kingdom of God is a Kingdom of light.

Darkness, death, sin, and satan do not reside in the Kingdom of God. Jesus reigns, and His Kingdom is a Kingdom of LIGHT and LOVE.

> *For He rescued us from the domain of darkness, and transferred us to the kingdom of His beloved Son.* (Colossians 1:13 NASB)

> *This is the message we have heard from Him and announce to you, that God is Light, and in Him, there is no darkness at all.* (1 John 1:5 NASB)

When Adam sinned, we were removed from the joy of living in God's presence. As a result, kingdoms on earth sprang up as man-centered, and they always ended up cruel, painful, and anti-God. These kingdoms' fruits were inequality, oppression, racism, disease, starvation, slavery, and death.

God's Kingdom is free of all such rotten fruit.

> *For the kingdom of God is not eating and drinking, but righteousness and peace and joy in the Holy Spirit.* (Romans 14:17 NASB)

Whether on earth or in the heavens, whether the material world or the spirit world, all belongs to Him and fills His Kingdom with righteousness, peace, joy, contentment, and love.

The message of the Kingdom of God is one of hope, thanksgiving, and rejoicing. It is a message of repentance and of returning to God, the Father, from our wayward Adamic state to the original state of fellowship with a loving Father as a coheir with His son in His Kingdom. It is a message of love—unequaled love by a Father who forgives and forgets our decision to turn from Him but welcomes us with open arms, a new robe, and ring, into His Kingdom to rule and reign with Him.

> *This is love: He loved us long before we loved him. It was his love, not ours. He proved it by sending his Son to be the pleasing sacrificial offering to take away our sins.* (1 John 4:10 TPT)

Being in perfect harmony with the Creator is the difference between *going to church* and *being the church*. The *Ekklesia* is not a building; it is you and me and all the other saints down through all the generations—past, present, and future—from across the globe. All those who have exercised their *free will* to accept Jesus as Lord and Master will reside within the Kingdom. Jesus brought the Kingdom with Him and *established it* here on earth.

How we have missed His message!

And *the fault for this lies mainly at the doorstep of church leadership*, which has failed to understand and teach God's intention and purpose but instead have either stopped and parked at the *salvation* Gospel or took detours into humanistic and worldly arenas. Much of Christianity today has become sidetracked from the things of Christ and has lost contact with CHRIST Himself. Worldly detours such as social justice, racial equality, and self-help programs can all too easily become a detour, *distracting us away from the person of Christ to the things of the world*.

Overall, the church—the structure, layout, atmosphere, format, rituals, speakers, etc.—have replaced the gathering of believers just to glorify Christ. As such, *coupled with the dismissal of the Holy Spirit's guiding and developing the church*, it has lost its authority, authenticity, and power. It stands as no more than another "social" experiment—a shiny car, with lots of bells and whistles, but no fuel, going nowhere.

We live amid a world consisting of kingdoms, both material and spiritual, each vying and clawing for recognition and authenticity. Satan has deceived the world (and the church) into believing that he has the authority and the control over our present world.

He does not.

God is in charge and has never relinquished authority or power to satan. Adam temporarily gave his authority and power to satan, but God never did. Jesus stripped satan of his apparent authority and power and holds all in His hands. He offers it to us; we only need to take it.

The *Ultimate Purpose* of God's *plan* is the establishment of the *Kingdom of God*. In fact, it is fair to say that the *Ultimate Purpose* of creation is the Kingdom of God—they are one and the same.

Recall Paul's revelation of God's mystery:

> *Just as He chose us in Him before the foundation of the world, that we would be holy and blameless before Him. In love, He predestined us to adoption as sons and daughters through Jesus Christ to Himself, according to the good pleasure of His will* (stage one of the kingdom). *He made known to us the mystery of His will, according to His good pleasure which He set forth in Him, regarding His plan of the fullness of the times, to bring all things together in Christ, things in the heavens and things on the earth. In Him we also have obtained an inheritance, having been predestined according to the purpose of Him who works all things in accordance with the plan of His will* (stage two of the kingdom). (Ephesians 1:4–5, 9–13 NASB)

God's *will* is His *Ultimate Purpose*. The "Kingdom come" is His will. They are one and the same. Jesus is the King, and all of creation is the Kingdom. Jesus came to reclaim the earthly portion of God's Kingdom from satan, who had it handed to him by Adam. That reclaiming began with the cross and will be completed with His second coming. Satan will be bound and removed for a thousand years while the *Kingdom of God* rules and reigns the earth. He will be released and allowed one last desperate attempt to regain power before being removed once and for all, along with the last rebellious humans.

Then the *will* of the Father will be established as His *"sons and daughters"* share and expand His *love* and *glory* throughout the universe.

By accepting Christ as Lord and Master, the *Kingdom* is advanced. The Holy Spirit takes up residence inside of us, dwelling in His temple.

Holy Spirit gives us knowledge, understanding, and power to BE the *Kingdom of God* amid a crooked and perverse generation of worldly kingdoms. He enables us to be the *Kingdom's* bright light in a dark world.

> *For indeed, the kingdom of God is within you.*
> (Luke 17:21 NKJV)

> *And as you go, preach, saying, "The kingdom of heaven is at hand." Heal the sick, cleanse the lepers, raise the dead, cast out demons. Freely you have received, freely give.* (Matthew 10:7–8 NKJV)

> *For the kingdom of God does not consist of food and drink, but righteousness, peace, and joy in the Holy Spirit.* (Romans 14:17 NKJV)

So initially, the Kingdom of God resides within us—those who believe in the LORD JESUS—in our spirits, in our worldview, and in how we choose to live our lives. Someday soon, OUR LORD will return, and the Kingdom will be fully established on earth, and *He will reign and rule over all the kingdoms of the world.*

*For it is written: "As I live, says the L*ORD*, every knee shall bow to Me, and every tongue shall confess to God."* (Romans 14:11 NKJV)

Until that day, we bring the Kingdom to earth with our spirits and our life.

CHAPTER 13

THE *EKKLESIA*[17]

And I tell you that you are Peter, and on this rock I will build My church, and the gates of Hades shall not prevail against it. (Matthew 16:18 MEV)

It is never a good thing when governments take control of faith-based beliefs. This is especially true of monarchies and dictatorships. When such organizations can control people's hearts in addition to controlling their minds, any hope of God's light breaking through the nation is extinguished. It will only be by extreme suffering, pain, and death that the King's advancement can occur. This has happened numerous times in history with the Gospel of the Kingdom.

Such was the case in 1602 when King James I of England put together a council of forty-seven scholars to translate the Holy Scriptures into English. Translations in English had already been done. Beginning with William Tyndale in 1522 (who was strangled and burned to death in 1536 for doing it), followed by the Geneva Bible in 1599 (which was an "unauthorized" translation used extensively by the Puritans and the Pilgrims).

Unfortunately, these translations did not sit well with King James. He was a monarch, and he insisted that the "National" Bible

---

17 For identification purposes, *E* is capitalized when referring to the kingdom of God Ekklesia.

for the state religion of Anglican Christianity support his position of *"the divine right of kings,"* which meant that no matter what he did or said, he was right. There would be no one over him—no pope, no bishop, no one—in or out of the church.

The translation was released in 1611 as the King James Authorized Version, and it was, and remains to this day, one of the most beautiful and accurate translations ever produced. In all fairness and honesty, the King James Version translation has done more to advance individual ownership and understanding of Scripture than any other translation.

But that does not mean it does not have some serious flaws and issues.

One such issue had to do with the word translated as *church*. Upon commissioning the council, King James gave them a list of fifteen directives required to be followed in doing their translation. An essential item on the list was that the Greek word *ekklesia* must always be translated as "church." By 1602, when the council was commissioned, the word *church* in England had come to mean a *"religious building or structure, supported by a staff of clergy and priests."*

The *church* was under King James's dominion as monarch, and if you disagreed with his theology, you would be tortured or executed. He was the *final* word on all *church* functions, activities, doctrines, rituals, etc.

With the significant influence that the British Empire held worldwide during the seventeenth and eighteenth centuries, this concept has become the norm. Even Bible translations that followed used this definition. To this day, *ekklesia* has been translated as *church*, and in most minds, translators and readers alike, this equates to a *building or structure for religious services with clergy*. This single word translation was one of the major reasons the Pilgrims left England and ended up in the New World.

Jesus only used the term twice. Notice in the language of the scripture noted at the beginning of this chapter, Jesus did not say *"upon this rock will I build my temple"* or *"will I build my synagogue."* Think about it; if He were speaking of a *church* such as King James wanted to be defined, one of those words is what He would have used.

But He did not, and what He did say was

> And on this rock I will build My Ekklesia,
> and the gates of Hades shall not prevail against it.
> (Matthew 16:18 MEV)

Ekklesia does not mean *church* as we know or think of it, and if not *church* as we know it, what was Jesus talking about?

The *Ekklesia*

When Jesus told his disciples that He was going to build His *Ekklesia*, there are two things that we know for sure:

1. They knew exactly what He was talking about.
2. They were totally taken aback—either out of confusion or excitement (perhaps a little of both).

Before we go any further, let us clear up one area that has caused great confusion and misunderstanding down through the centuries. Jesus was NOT telling Peter that He was going to build His *Ekklesia* on *Peter*. He was telling Peter that it was on the *revelation that Jesus was the Son of God* that Peter had gotten that the *Ekklesia* would be built upon. Jesus is the "rock." The Apostle Peter had a significant role in founding Christianity, but He is not the "rock" the *pope* or any other titled man desires to give to him. It is all about Jesus—no one else.

Recall back in chapter 10, "Thy Kingdom Come," we discussed Daniel's prophecies concerning the empires of the world and the Kingdom of God coming as a "*stone*" broken from the "*mountain*" that would crush all worldly kingdoms and would endure forever.

> And in the days of those kings, the God of
> heaven will set up a kingdom which will never be

destroyed, and that kingdom will not be left for another people; it will crush and put an end to all these kingdoms, but it will itself endure forever. Just as you saw that a stone (rock) was broken off from the mountain without hands and that it crushed the iron, the bronze, the clay, the silver, and the gold. (Daniel 2:44 NKJV)

Then the iron, the clay, the bronze, the silver, and the gold were crushed to pieces all at the same time, and they were like chaff from the summer threshing floors, and the wind carried them away so that not a trace of them was found. But the stone (rock) that struck the statue became a great mountain and filled the entire earth. (Daniel 2:35 NKJV)

Jesus said to the Pharisees:

And he who falls on this stone (rock) will be broken to pieces; but on whomever it (rock) falls, it will scatter him like dust. (Matthew 21:44 NKJV)

Now add Jesus's declaration to Peter to these prophecies:

And I tell you that you are Peter, and on this rock I will build My Ekklesia and the gates of Hades shall not prevail against it. (Matthew 16:18 MEV)

The *Kingdom of God* will become a great mountain that will fill the entire earth:

Then the seventh angel sounded; and there were loud voices in heaven, saying, "The kingdom of the world has become the kingdom of our Lord and of His Christ; and He will reign forever and ever." (Revelation 11:15 NKJV)

Jesus was saying, The Kingdom has arrived…because Jesus had arrived, and He was bringing the Kingdom with Him. The *ekklesia* is all about government—not *church* as we think of it.

> *For a child will be born to us, a son will be given to us, And the government will rest on His shoulders; And His name will be called Wonderful Counselor, Mighty God, Eternal Father, Prince of Peace. There will be no end to the increase of His government or peace, On the throne of David and over his kingdom, to establish it and to uphold it with justice and righteousness from then on and forevermore.* (Isaiah 9:6–7 NASB)

And the disciples understood that completely.

The term *ekklesia*[18] has its roots in the Greek Hellenistic Empire and was adopted by the Romans that followed them.

The word *ekklesia* means

> *an assembly of people called out for a particular purpose; a governmental gathering to enact law; an assembly to represent the Empire.*

In secular terms, it meant whenever two or more Roman citizens were assembled, they had the authority to represent the emperor and make local law and maintain order.

So when Jesus said,

> *For where two or three are assembled in My name, there I am in their midst* (Matthew 18:20 MEV),

---

[18] https://www.britannica.com/topic/Ecclesia-ancient-Greek-assembly.

they understood exactly what He meant. They lived under the weight of Roman Law, and the *ekklesia* was a widely known and used method for Rome to maintain control throughout the Empire. They also knew Daniel's prophecies and were waiting and expecting David's Kingdom (Israel) to be restored throughout the world. They understood that the promised *Messiah* was to be that *stone* and *deliverer*. So when Jesus told them what He did, they knew what He was talking about, and that is why they asked this question just before He ascended to the Father:

> *Therefore, when they had come together, they asked Him, saying, "Lord, will You at this time restore the kingdom to Israel?"* (Acts 1:6 MEV)

Many laugh at their *"lack"* of understanding regarding this question saying the apostles still did not understand what Jesus's mission was. They are wrong to laugh. The apostles understood perfectly. They were expecting the advancement of the earthly Kingdom because Jesus has given them a reason to. (Notice in His answer, Jesus never denies what they are asking but only tells them it is not for them to know the timing.) The question was not misplaced; it was only too narrow in scope. They did not understand that God's Kingdom was not limited to Israel but included the entire world.

There are instances in the *Diary* where we see the ekklesia in play. For example, in the Book of Acts,[19] we see where a *"silversmith"* riot in Ephesus was controlled and squelched because *citizens* were able to invoke *civil (ekklesia) law.*

What does *Ekklesia* mean to the *Kingdom*?

In a nutshell? Everything.

We will answer the question with a question: *Why was the early church so successful in its phenomenal growth?*

---

[19] Acts 19:21–41.

How could literally *thousands* of people convert so quickly, to the point that all of Jerusalem was in upheaval? How did Paul reach hundreds of thousands of people, *planting assemblies* everywhere he went, leaving them with *solid leadership* after only a few days of teaching and instruction?

The Book of Acts uses such words as

> so that all who lived in Asia heard the word of
> the Lord Jesus, both Jews, and Greeks. (Acts 19:10
> MEV)

By historical accounts, that "*all*" is over a million people Paul reached in Asia (without a TV show), and from a *tent-making* shop no less!

And

> by the power of the Spirit of God, so that from
> Jerusalem and as far around as Illyricum, I have
> fully preached the gospel of Christ. (Romans 15:19
> MEV)

This covered the entire area of Asia-Minor with converts and *church* plantings everywhere he went.

They had no seminaries, no Bible colleges (no Bibles for that matter), no cell phones, no computers, no automobiles, buses, or airplanes. They traveled by walking on foot hundreds of miles, and they talked with hundreds of people. That was all they had to work with. They were unwanted most times, persecuted, physically assaulted, jailed, and eventually executed. Yet they turned the known world completely upside down!

But they went forth with two things that have been, for the most part, overlooked in modern evangelism and missionary endeavors:

1. The Holy Spirit
2. The *Ekklesia*

God's *Plan* is NOT to create "churches"—buildings, structures, a rigid clergy, rituals, indulgences, entertainment. No, that is *religion*. You may not believe this, but Jesus did not come to establish a *religion* or *to plant churches*. Man does that—not God.

Jesus came to reestablish the *relationship* between the FATHER and His children. Jesus came to bring the KINGDOM OF GOD to earth.

The HOLY SPIRIT is the POWER and the ANOINTING behind the KINGDOM OF GOD.

The *Ekklesia* is people taking the Kingdom of God into their spheres of influence—into the *marketplace*, their family, their work, entertainment, school, social life, etc., places and areas where they interact with others. It does not depend on *trained* specialists, clergy, and buildings. The *Ekklesia* was a movement of people taking the King and His Kingdom into the world with the power and the anointing of the Holy Spirit.

It was not "planting churches"; it was "planting people" filled with the Holy Spirit.

What about today?

Watching most YouTube Christian programs, reading most Christian books and magazines, and attending most Evangelical and Pentecostal churches, it is disturbing to discover just how much the present-day *Christian church* is centered on the church structure and *man*-based activities. The underlying message is that God's primary concern is the building and church activities involved and how that will result in *redemption* and *happiness for the members*.

The overwhelming theme of today's church in America is the *easy conversion*. You know what we mean—*heads bowed down with no one looking (heaven forbid if anyone should be embarrassed)*. Then everyone in the sanctuary (sinner, saved, preacher alike) all recite (so no one is *singled out*) the *sinner's prayer*. At the most, please fill out this little card so we know if anyone got *saved* or not and drop it anonymously in the box on your way out. Then dismissal to go home and catch the Sunday football game.

Each Sunday, there is a socially redeeming feel good *"how to live the good, abundant and prosperous Christian life"* pep talk while we wait for the Lord to come and carry us away to our *deserved* reward in heaven. The songs, the conversations, the sermons, the offerings, and the invitations all revolve around the promise that God is acutely aware of our needs and desires and that He has a readily available plan to meet them—today—probably before we leave the service to rush home for the game!

Is that carrying out the *Ultimate Purpose and Plan* God has for us? Is that our purpose in Christ? To fill a seat every Sunday morning for one and a half hours (or less) and then basically, for all intents and purposes, forget about God the rest of the week except for maybe saying grace at dinnertime?

It seems a far cry from *"all of heaven rejoicing"* in the salvation of one lost sheep.

That is *religion*—and *feel-good religion* at that. That is not *relationship*. If you treated your spouse that way, it would not be long before you would be headed to divorce court. Unfortunately, many "Christians" today have already been to *God's "divorce court,"* and the sad news is that they do not even know they have been there.

The fact remains that around 90 percent of the people who claim Jesus as their Savior never change how they live. If what we claim does not make a difference in our lives, then it is only carnal knowledge. It is just *stuff—religion*. It means nothing. It is not who we are. Jesus came to *transform us*—to change us—from worldly, carnal-minded individuals into *God-centered, Kingdom-focused sons and daughters.*

The most *successful* churches since the '80s are the *megachurches and the seeker-friendly churches.* They have "success"—as measured by the *world's standard,* using variables such as congregation size, offerings, and building structures. But do they operate under the power and presence of the Holy Spirit?

In other words, do they *change* people, or do they *accommodate* people?

The differences between the *church* of today and the *Ekklesia* that helps us know the AWE and the FATHERHOOD of God is illustrated by the following table:

God-Man Model	Man-God Model
God the Father	God the Master
Internal	External
Spirit	Flesh
Life-giving	Life pleasing
Unto Him—blessing to Him	Unto me—favor for me
Interdependence	Self-reliance
The law of love	The love of law
Unconditional love	Personal achievement
Humility	Competition
Unity	Individual success
Love covers/restoration	Love for recognition
Respect and honor	Distrust and disrespect
Lay down your life	Conditional, selfish love
A Son of God	A slave to me
The Father's unconditional love	Personal ambition

We are so focused on ourselves that we do not see the Father's focus on His Son. He has a purpose for His Son being released in the earth, bringing the *redemptive* story along with it, but a purpose that goes beyond the *redemption story* to His original and ultimate intent of family, an intent that has been largely ignored by the *church* and the shepherds over them.

Understand us; we are not saying *redemption* is a "faulty" message—far from it. Redemption is not only the *right* message, but it is the critical part of God's plan. We are saying that too much of Christianity has *kept the message and discarded the plan.*

The prodigal son must first be redeemed and returned home before the "family" comes together as one. *But once home, the family becomes the message of the plan.*

The *temple church* has an important role, and it is not our intent to trash the *church.* It is a focal point for assembly, instruction, and activities. It is a bastion of fellowship and mutual support. It serves the community and rallies the elect into evangelism and outreach. *The issue is all about church versus Ekklesia—it is about focus.* In the vast majority of *temple churches,* the focus is on the building, the programs, the routine and ritual, the worship, the entertainment; in summary, on the *things of Christ* and not on the *person of Christ.* The focus must be on Jesus—period. Everything else is secondary. The key players are the people, the *assembly together of two or three*—the *Ekklesia*—not the clergy. Unfortunately, the vast majority of *temple churches* have it just the opposite, focusing on the "worship entertainment" and high profile, charismatic speakers while the people only attend like so many bystanders. Looking at the typical *church* from the outside, they look more like "holding centers" where the people hunker down in the sanctuary for ninety minutes waiting for liberation. Yet it is the people—the Ekklesia—who will bring the hungry into the fold.

The *Kingdom will not—and has not—advanced under church conditions.* The Holy Spirit does not operate that way. Look today where the most incredible growth in the Kingdom is occurring, places like China, Iran, and Iraq, places where the *temple church* is not germane (or even in existence). Still the Holy Spirit and the *Ekklesia* are moving and winning souls.

The next and final *Great Awakening* in America will not come until there is a *"great falling away"* from the dependence on the *temple church* and rejuvenation of the *"body of Christ."* There is an intense desire in the young generations to *find* something substantial in this world. They see superficial, phoniness and temporal, fleeting *Hollywood* love, happiness, and peace. They *yearn for something real to cling to.* That something is God. Because society has taken God out of their lives, their inner spirits cry out for God. When the *churches* get their *act* together with the Holy Spirit—and the congregations become the Ekklesias in the marketplace—these generations will break the doors down, running to their Creator.

There is nothing wrong with *temple church*—until it replaces the *Ekklesia*.

God designed His plan around the Ekklesia and the Holy Spirit. That is not our word, that is God's. Read it for yourself—the Book of Acts. There is the template—the Holy Spirit's template. It is what worked for the *early rain* movement, and it is what will work for the *latter rain* movement as well. That movement is just around the corner, ready to *burst* forth.

The problem with the *temple church* is it can become the central thought of our Christian life, and instead of being occupied with Him—Yeshua—and His life and Gospel of the Kingdom, we are occupied with the *church* and ourselves. As a result, we miss Him totally. Not all; this is not a blanket condemnation of all *churches* or any denomination, but it is rampant enough so that the Spirit is grieved and quenched.

Yes, there are many good, Holy Spirit-filled *churches* trying their hardest to bring God to the people, but for every one of them, there are seven of these others.

With the focus on the *temple church*, it is all about us being happy and God being a good God because He is always thinking about us. We honestly believe that everything here is about us and our happiness and our delight in living. *"Life—and more abundantly"* is the modern Christian manta. Absent is any thinking that there are sacrifices and suffering. That is a foreign concept in our Western way of thinking about God. Never in the history of the *church* in America has there been such constant *church jumping*. As a result, fewer "Christians" are satisfied with their *church* and are ready to jump if the curtains' color is not to their liking. The majority of *church growth* consists of people moving from congregation to congregation. Meanwhile, the "marketplace" continues along without knowing Christ.

172

As discussed earlier, the Triune Godhead formed a *Plan* of Their *Ultimate Intention*. Look back to our earlier analogy of the architect and builder. What would happen if the builder got his plans mixed up and began building from the wrong set of plans? It would be a disaster! The builder may build a structure all right, but it would not be what the architect wanted to be built.

To a large degree, that is what has happened to Christianity. God made His *Ultimate Purpose and Plan*, and man has been building from the wrong set of plans. Instead of focusing on and building what God desired and wanted—His *Kingdom of sons* on earth, via the Ekklesia—we have focused on and built "churches" (buildings and structures), rituals, rites, doctrines, programs, and man-centered social justice movements. Most of these are not bad things on their own merits, but they are not the Gospel message of the *Kingdom* that Yeshua brought to the earth. Yeshua brought a single *Kingdom*-oriented message of sonship for all of humankind. Now over forty thousand independent denominations are claiming their own revelation version of His message and condemning the other 39,999 as being in error.

Let's all get back to a few essential things. God is central in the universe. His vital FATHERHOOD is the controlling factor that determined His plan, purpose, and intention for *all things*. At this point, He, the Father, begins to open His hidden place to let us see how His Son is related to this glorious eternal purpose. This eternal purpose is to have "sons and daughters" to go into eternity with Him and share His LOVE and GLORY.

Father God is in heaven, and he desires that earth would be an expression of heaven on earth. So He sent Jesus to empty Himself of everything of who He was in heaven—all His pleasures, honors, and blessings—and He was sent to the earth to show and bring about an impartation on earth so that the Son would have the preeminence in the earth about everything. What we call the Lord's Prayer is a mighty expression of His desire to have earth become what heaven is.

Let's not confine to four walls, once a week what is designed to be a 24/7 people movement out in the marketplace, the workplace, the school, the gym, transforming society, cities, and nations. Let's not restrict *ministry* to professionally trained specialists and ministers. Every *believer* is a minister of God's truth:

> *He gave some to be apostles, prophets, evangelists, pastors, and teachers, for the equipping of the saints, for the work of service, and for the building up of the body of Christ, until we all come into the unity of the faith and of the knowledge of the Son of God, into a complete man, to the measure of the stature of the fullness of Christ, so we may no longer be children, tossed here and there by waves and carried about with every wind of doctrine by the trickery of men, by craftiness with deceitful scheming. But, speaking the truth in love, we may grow up in all things into Him, who is the head, Christ Himself, from whom the whole body is joined together and connected by every joint and ligament, as every part effectively does its work and grows, building itself up in love.* (Ephesians 4:11–16 MEV)

The movement is fluid and expansive. It grows where there is a spontaneous movement of the *Power* and the *Anointing* of the Holy Spirit!

Combined with the word of our testimony, people become *transformed*, and *their lives are changed*. That is the *Ultimate Intention, Purpose, and Plan* of the FATHER—to change people's lives so they become the *Blessed, Loved Children* of God going into eternity.

The world has changed dramatically in the past months, and greater change is on the horizon. God is calling His remnant—the *Ekklesia*—to stand up and be the bride for the groom. The time is now to prepare ourselves for the "Awakening" and harvest that will follow.

The *temple church* supports the *Ekklesia;* the *Ekklesia* changes the world.

The *Ekklesia* is *the church.*

Together they will bring the final Great Awakening to the world.

The world is not looking for *church*; there are thousands of them. The world is seeking a *relationship* with its Creator. That *relationship* is demonstrated and found in the *Ekklesia*.

The Holy Spirit knows the template that works. It is up to the "remnant" to implement His template in the marketplace. That is where *true* redemption, salvation, and transformation occurs.

We will do the greatest service for the next generation of Christians by passing on to them the highest concept of God that our Hebrew and Christian fathers passed on to us.

For further reading and study on the EKKLESIA, we recommend the following:

- *Ekklesia* and *Transformation*, both by Ed Silvoso
- *Leaving Church Becoming Ekklesia* by Tim Kurtz
- *Letters to the Church* by Francis Chan

CHAPTER 14

FOR SUCH A *TIME* AS THIS

<u>What *Time* is it anyway?</u>

We have seen how the Triune God, driven by His unshakeable love, wanted to share all that He had with a physical creation. We had seen how this desire was developed into a *plan* by the *council before the foundations of the world were laid*, a plan whereby humans, *made in the image of God*, could experience and partake of God's goodness, peace, joy, and love and be given the undeserved, unmerited gift of redemption along with the invitation of *coreigning* alongside of Jesus in His kingdom. God sent His Son to the cross—willingly—to atone and pay for our poor decisions and misplaced pride. All that is required of us is to *receive* what He has offered. Receive the WORK of the cross and His Son as the only way to the FATHER. Accept the LIFE of the cross as our life every day going forward.

As mentioned in the introduction to this book, we find ourselves living in extraordinary times with many things occurring that the world has never seen before. There is a great fear among people about what the future holds. Worldwide pandemics, crazy politics, international economic chaos, wars, and worldwide terrorism have put the world on edge and full alert. There is a sense something big is happening and that what we are seeing is only the beginning.

We do not minimize those things. They are real, and they will probably get worse before they get better. Evil will attempt to control nations and send the world into a downward spiral of chaos and darkness. It is inevitable, and it is all laid out in the *Diary*. This world's *kingdoms* are under the dominion of evil, and men have allowed themselves to become the servants and slaves of the dark one.

So it is a time of *gloom and doom, fear and trembling, hunker down,* and *"Woe is us,"* right?

"No!" We answer back! And again we shout, "No!"

It is a time of rejoicing! Singing! And dancing!

Like Paul and Silas, it is a time of singing and praising God, a time of drawing nearer to the Creator and feel His love for us like never before.

Why do we say this? Because we honor evil and darkness? Because we are pleased there is so much chaos and upheaval? No—a thousand times NO. We honor good and peace. We honor God who is good and light. And the light shines the brightest in the darkest of night. God is in charge, and we know that.

> *All things work together for good to those who love God, to those who are called according to His purpose.* (Romans 8:28 MEV)

Remember what this *Earth Age* is for. It is for *believers* to draw closer to our FATHER. It is for *children* to mature into *sons and daughters* and earn their *eternal inheritance.* It is for *lovers of God* to walk and live as *lovers of God,* to "pick up our cross" and follow our Lord. It is for *harvesters* to go out into the fields and harvest.

"For such a time as this," we were placed here by our God. Why? Because this is the time He needs us. These are the days when His remnant rises and proclaims the Gospel of the Living God to a dark world. It is *for such a time as this* that God's *diamonds* sparkle and reflect His pure light out into a dark world to show them the way, to show them the LOVE of the FATHER. And when we allow the Holy Spirit to be the POWER behind our *reflection,* the light is like a bright lighthouse beam lighting the way to the FATHER.

We do not know the details of what lies ahead, the hows and whens of it, but we know the whole of it. We know evil will increase along with the darkness it brings. We know there will be famines, pestilences, and starvation. We know lawlessness will increase, and hearts will grow colder. We know there will be wars and global destruction. We know there will be a great falling away from the Gospel and that many false prophets and doctrines shall rise. We know that there will be global persecution of the *believers* and that many will die for their faith. We know the world will be taken in by an *Antichrist* who will deceive many and usher in a *one-world* government. We know all these things because they are written in the *Diary*.

Yes, these are all ugly things that no one wishes on anyone, but none of this is unknown to us—none of it should surprise us. For years, we have talked about the "*last days*" and the end. Well, it appears they are coming at us like a freight train, and we are standing in the middle of the track looking them square in the face as it roars and rumbles, spewing black smoke and squealing fire, bearing down on us. It is true "*no man knows the day or the hour*," but we are to know the "*seasons*," and the odds that we will get out of the 2020s decade without seeing some of these things happening is looking pretty slim.

We could be *politically correct* and not mention these things and allow the reader to feel comfortable and at ease with their "*walk*" with Christ right now. But we cannot do that—eternity for many is on the line right now.

Is there a *silver lining* in all this?

Yes!

This time will not last forever. It too shall pass, but *what WE do during this time will last for eternity.*

This is the atmosphere when the Holy Spirit moves. For one purpose, these things and events turn people's hearts to seek the FATHER and turn from their evil ways to HIM. It is the time of the final Great Awakening.

And we, all of us who believe—the *Remnant*—are the messengers put here by God to spread the *Word*, to reap the harvest. It is not a *silver lining* but an honor to be chosen as such.

When asked, Jesus said,

> *For then there will be a great tribulation, such as has not occurred since the beginning of the world until now, nor ever will again. And if those days had not been cut short, no life would have been saved; but for the sake of the elect those days will be cut short.* (Matthew 24:21–22 NASB)

We have been given a great honor. For two thousand years, Christianity has spread across the globe, continent by continent, nation by nation, slowly being preached to the world. Jesus said once it has "*been preached in all the world—and then the end will come.*"

As Christianity approaches that final stage, God has selected those chosen ones to see it through its ultimate Earth Age finale. We believe that is us—the Remnant—at this time, rising across the globe, in many lands and nations, standing for Christ, making their voices heard, filled with the *Anointing* and *Power* of the Holy Spirit. Just like the early believers who *caught* the Gospel of the kingdom from Jesus, we're *handpicked* by the FATHER for such a mighty task of getting the Gospel planted into the Earth Age. We are also *handpicked* by the FATHER to wrap up the Earth Age with a magnificent harvest. Yes, some will experience the *suffering* side of the age, while others experience the *miracles and revival side*. But whatever side one ends up, we are one *glorified*, united Ekklesia!

These times only bring us closer to Him. *We need always to keep our eyes on HIM and not on the world.* Do not allow the world to distract you, to pull you away from the great and wonderful calling you have. The world will do what it will do. Do not be alarmed, worried, or troubled by what you see happening. God is not taken by surprise by what the world does, and neither should we be. It is all temporary, fleeting, and will pass. It means only two things to us:

1. There is a great movement of God coming where millions will come to our Lord!
2. THE KING IS COMING!

And HE is bringing His Kingdom with Him, the one we get to be "coheirs" with.

We already know what tomorrow's *headlines* will be. They do not bother us. They only usher in His *glory* for all the world to witness. What He said will happen—*is happening.* Okay, *so what?*

> Let the redeemed of the LORD say so, Whom He
> has redeemed from the hand of the enemy. (Psalm
> 107:2 NKJV)

So satan has shown his cards, and evil men have sided with him. Okay...

So he roams about like a lion, seeking whom he may devour. Okay...

So nations and governments rise up that stand against the God of creation. Okay...

Are you ready? All together now, on three.

"One..."
"Two..."
"Three..."
"Let the redeemed of the Lord say, 'Soooo?'"

We are the "redeemed of the Lord," and we look at such posturing and antics of satan, and we collectively say, *"So?"* We are children of the Most High God, the very God who not only created satan but who reigns and rules and is in total and complete charge of all things—always has been, always will be.

There is no cause for us to be fearful. There is no need for us to tremble at satan's posturing. We are children of God, and *"for such a time as this,"* we are here. Our God chose us to be here now because He not only needed us to be here at this time, but He knew He could depend upon us to fulfill the mission He has for us at this time. What is that mission? The HARVEST. We have been chosen to participate in the greatest harvest ever seen in the history of Christianity.

So...what time is it?

It is time for the remnant—the body of Christ, the bride, the *Ekklesia*—to

> *arise, shine; For your light has come! And the glory of the LORD is risen upon you.* (Isaiah 60:1 NKJV)

How do we rise up?

> *Therefore take up the whole armor of God, that you may be able to withstand in the evil day, and having done all, to stand.* (Ephesians 6:13 NKJV)

The Purpose of this *Time*

The world is entering what is commonly referred to as "*the last days.*" Jesus prophesized them, as did many others. The *Ekklesia* has talked about them, sung about them, and wrote about them for hundreds of years. They have been expected, anticipated, and wrongly identified for centuries. It certainly looks like they are now arriving. All the signs are there, and it is clear the world is near its *breaking point*. It simply cannot continue on this path much longer without completely falling apart.

Yes, there will be a "*great falling away.*" Many of the established churches will fold from lack of being grounded in God's Word and promises. Yes, there will be persecution and anti-Christ activities toward those who remain faithful. Yes, there will be deceptions, false messiahs, and distorted doctrines. Yes, there will be suffering for the cause and sake of our Lord. All that is in the *Diary*, and the *Holy Spirit* has given us a *heads-up*. Whatever happens during this Earth Age is temporary. It will pass, and eternity begins.

And we need not fear. We need not worry.

> *Be anxious for nothing, but in everything by prayer and supplication, with thanksgiving, let your*

requests be made known to God. (Philippians 4:6 NKJV)

Because there will also be a *Great Awakening*—a massive movement of souls to seek and find their Creator, their Redeemer, their Savior. While there will be a "great falling away," we believe many other *established* churches will become renewed in God's Word and will turn to the Holy Spirit for direction and guidance. Millions of people across the planet will cry out to God and seek His face. God needs His harvesters ready to bring in the harvest. And we are here to be part of that great harvest as we swing our harvesting sickle through the ripe harvest. Our Lord commands us to harvest:

> *"Go therefore and make disciples of all the nations, baptizing them in the name of the Father and of the Son and of the Holy Spirit, teaching them to observe all things that I have commanded you; and lo, I am with you always, even to the end of the age." Amen.* (Matthew 28:19–20 NKJV)

God could have placed you back in the medieval centuries—in the 1300s. He did not. Because He knew you were needed now—in the twenty-first century. This is the time when God needs all His *best harvesters.* And he promises that HE is with you always! Even to the very end! *What is there to fear or worry about* if the *Creator and* LORD *of all Creation is with you?*

It is not a time to cower or hide but to rejoice and give praise to the King of heaven.

The signs also mean that the time is short to our Lord's return. It truly is getting closer to the day when He will return in the clouds, and His Kingdom will be established on earth. Again, what an honor to be chosen to be here for the most remarkable event of Earth Age history!

All of this makes it an exciting time to be a son and daughter of God! The King is coming!

There is a purpose to all that is happening. No, God is not the author of chaos, evil, and death. He offers peace, goodness, and life. God desires to have a *voluntary family* to go into eternity with. Many have chosen otherwise, and as a result, darkness covers much of the earth.

But always keep one thing in mind: *darkness has no power*. You do not turn on the *dark* switch in your house to create darkness; you turn OFF the light switch. Light holds the energy—the power. Darkness is nothing more than the absence of light. Darkness is a fraud, a mask. It has no power, only the façade of deception and lies.

In this day and age, our job is to turn ON the light switch—to sow the *truth*.

> *The light shines in the darkness, but the darkness has not overcome it.* (John 1:5 MEV)

You Are Special to FATHER

You were born…*"for such a time as this."* FATHER loves you dearly and deeply, and *He also loves all those out there who do not know Him yet*. He desires, beyond any other desire, for you to be His light and to *lead* them to HIM. He placed you here to *"shine" His light on their pathway*.

This is the PLAN of the FATHER. His PLAN is for His children to mature into *"sons" of God* and be the bride of Christ and be "coheirs" with Jesus Christ in the Kingdom, to be priests and ministers to the lost of the world.

Why? Because His LOVE is so big, so all-encompassing, so overwhelming. HE wants ALL to come into the Kingdom. He desires NONE to perish. His *sons and daughters* are the ones to carry the Kingdom's Gospel into all the world to reach the world.

If not us, then who?

God works through people. The Holy Spirit will convict and draw people to Jesus, but that is in conjunction with people spreading the Gospel. Jesus's last words on earth were

> *But you shall receive power when the Holy*
> *Spirit comes upon you. And you shall be My wit-*
> *nesses in Jerusalem, and in all Judea and Samaria,*
> *and to the ends of the earth.* (Acts 1:8 MEV)

FATHER needs you now—more than ever. You are special to God; you have a mission—a calling, a calling that goes far beyond the fears and concerns of this fallen world.

Jesus is coming for His bride, a bride without spot or wrinkle, a bride that has prepared herself and is ready and able to meet her bridegroom. That bride will be found ready. We are that bride. How does the *bride* prepare herself? By "working" the harvest fields, not by sitting around primping herself. The more the *bride* works the harvest field, the more beautiful she is to the groom.

We live amid a world of kingdoms, each vying and clawing for recognition and authenticity. Satan holds control over them, so initially, the kingdom of God resides within us—those who believe in the LORD JESUS—in our spirits, in our worldview, and in how we choose to live our lives. Someday, very soon, OUR LORD will return and fully establish the kingdom on earth, and *He will reign and rule over all the kingdoms of the world, and we will reign with HIM.*

The fears and worries of this world do not compare to the glory or what FATHER has in store for us:

> *For I consider that the sufferings of this pres-*
> *ent time are not worthy of being compared with*
> *the glory which shall be revealed to us. The eager*
> *expectation of the creation waits for the appearance*
> *of the sons of God. Creation itself also will be set*
> *free from its slavery to corruption into the glorious*
> *freedom of the children of God. We know that the*
> *whole creation groans and travails in pain together*
> *until now. Not only that, but we also, who have the*
> *firstfruits of the Spirit, groan within ourselves while*
> *eagerly waiting for adoption, the redemption of our*
> *bodies.* (Romans 8:18–23 MEV)

You are Part of God's Original Plan

The *Holy Spirit is the fuel—the power—*that *transforms* our "sparkling" diamonds into *powerful beacons of light,* blaring out into the darkness over a sea of floundering kingdoms denying its Creator.

Have you made that decision yet? Have you received God as your FATHER? IF you have not, what is stopping you? Weigh what has been presented and discussed in this book. Meditate on it. Test it in your heart; see if your spirit resonates with it. Search the innermost corners of your soul for the truth. God is real. God did all this—for you. He loves you so much HE was "*pleased*" to "*crush*" His Son, a horrible, torturous death, nailed to a cross, so that YOU could also become His child. God loved you before "*the foundations of the world were laid.*" Think about that. Allow those thoughts to penetrate your spirit. His plan of salvation and redemption…is for YOU.

You do not need a big splash, a magnificent altar call, or a special "news" alert. You only need to talk to your FATHER. HE waits for you. HE knows your heart. HE asks that you *confess* that you are a sinner. And HE asks that you *repent*—turn from living with *self* on the front burner and place HIM on your front burner. That is all HE asks. If you are feeling anything pulling on you, then that is the Holy Spirit speaking to you. Listen to Him; He is only speaking to you for your well-being.

Listen to this by the Apostle Paul:

> *For this reason, also God highly exalted Him, and bestowed on Him the name, which is above every name, so that at the name of Jesus every knee will bow, of those who are in heaven and on earth and under the earth, and that every tongue will confess that Jesus Christ is Lord, to the glory of God the Father.* (Philippians 2:9–11 NASB)

Did you catch that? Every knee will bow, every tongue will confess.

So you will do it sooner or later. Why not do so now and enjoy the LOVE of the FATHER?

<u>Welcome to the Kingdom!</u>

Being a child of the Kingdom, there are three things we ask you to do:

1. Develop a daily dialogue with your FATHER. Yes, we are talking about a *prayer* life. But we do not want to use that term because so many people get the concept of *prayer* confused with a recital, ritual, formal approach. Prayer is simply communicating with FATHER. It is just talking and listening to your FATHER. To the church at Ephesus, the Apostle Paul wrote for them to

    > *pray in the Spirit always with all kinds of prayer and supplication. To that end be alert with all perseverance and supplication for all the saints.* (Ephesians 6:18 MEV)

    Our first reaction to that is, *"How do I do that? I cannot spend the whole day on my knees saying prayers."*
    And you are right; you cannot, and Paul is not asking you to. Talking to God is no different than talking to your family all day. He wants us to interact with Him all day. Go ahead, talk to HIM about doing the laundry or cutting the grass. You will find out HE cares about every aspect of your life! Talk to Him right now! See if He does not know you are reading this book!
    He is our FATHER, and HE truly is there for everything.
    Prayer is communication—all day, more casual than formal—with your God. The Triune Godhead will tell you things. They will lead you. They will answer questions. They will navigate you through your daily life. *When you accept Jesus into your life, the GODHEAD shows up, moves in, and is there 24/7.* Now tell me that is not cool!
    And one more thing. Notice we said prayer is communication. Communication is a two-way street. It is not

only us asking FATHER for what we want. It is allowing FATHER to talk to us and tell us what HE wants. Prayer is listening to the voice of GOD as much, if not more so, than Him listening to us (besides, He already knows what we need, but we need to find out what HE needs). And this is truer now, going into these "*last days*," than ever before.

2. Begin a journey into the *Diary*—God's Word. Find a translation that does not *water* down the truth and begin bringing His Word into your heart and life. We suggest you start with the Gospels of Jesus—Matthew, Mark, Luke, and John—and allow the Holy Spirit to lead you from there. God gave us His *Diary*—His Word on everything. It is there for us. It is a gift. It is not a book of fairy tales or Jewish history or even world history. It is not a science book. No. It is the "living" WORD of God that the Holy Spirit inspired over forty different authors to write over fifteen centuries that all together tells the beautiful story of God's great plan for each of us. There is no other writing so blessed, so wonderful, so special. It is a blessing. Take it and hold it dear to your heart. Learn it, know it, and speak it. From it comes life.

3. Finally, find a Holy Spirit-led church and begin attending. While Christianity is an individual decision to accept Jesus Christ, God's plan is a corporate "body" united together as the "bride" of Christ. Unless you are John the Baptist, there are no *lone rangers* in Christianity.

> *Let us not forsake the assembling of ourselves together, as is the manner of some, but let us exhort one another, especially as you see the Day approaching.* (Hebrews 10:25 MEV)

We need one another. And as this current age progresses, that need will become more pronounced and evident *"for such a time as this."* As you progress with the Holy Spirit, you will find local, physical support from others of faith and global support and intercession via the Holy Spirit from believers around the world. Our *graduation* from this *Earth Age* will be the most amazing *corporate* event the world has ever witnessed, when all the *saints*, both past and present, of God receive their *"glorified"* bodies and rise in unison to meet our Lord—*"for such a time as this."* Until then, assemble and fellowship one with another.

Why stop at Salvation?

Salvation is the greatest gift God can give us. It is wonderful, priceless and unmerited, and abundantly loving. Once you accept Jesus as your life, you are *"born again"* as a child of the FATHER into the Kingdom. Hallelujah! The angels rejoice!

Salvation is not the end of the journey; it is but the beginning. The means for transformation by the renewing of your mind is made available to you. Take advantage of it. *Allow the Holy Spirit to enter your spirit and begin the tutoring process.*

Jesus closed the Book of Revelation with the following:

> *Behold, I am coming quickly, and My reward is with Me, to render to every man according to what he has done.* (Revelation 22:12 NASB)

The journey continues. We have a commission from our King—to be empowered by the Holy Spirit and to take the Gospel into all the world so that one day, soon, we will share in the Kingdom of God. You do not need to be a *missionary* to the deep jungles of Africa; you only need to be a *missionary* to the "marketplace"—your "marketplace."

That is our FATHER'S ULTIMATE INTENTION and PURPOSE. Sitting back waiting for the Lord's return is not.

Yes, we can do that if we wish to, but doing so puts us in disobedience to the FATHER'S commandment.

Why miss out on the harvest? Why miss out on the excitement of the *"last days"*? Why miss out on the *joy* and the *glory* of serving in these times? Why be a *spectator* when you can get in the game and be a *participant?*

What JOY missed when not being in "HIS GLORY"!

Yes, the tomb is empty—Praise God! But do not stop there. Move on. Your journey is not complete. Jesus did not stop there. HE ascended. HIS mission on earth was finished.

You too will ascend, but your mission on earth is not complete—not yet. Press on into the glory that God has planned for you. There is so much more for you! You will have all eternity to talk about it!

Move to the next step and be filled with the ANOINTING and the POWER of the Holy Spirit. Allow Him to *tutor* you. Allow your spirit to *play catch* with the Holy Spirit. You might be surprised what *pitches* He has for you!

The HARVEST awaits your sickle.

CHAPTER 15

FROM GLORY TO GLORY

There was a time before creation when the thing we know as *love* was embodied entirely in the Triune Godhead. Before the universe came into being, when only the Trinity existed, the FATHER loved the SON; the SON loved the FATHER. They shared Their love all during the eons before creation through the HOLY SPIRIT.

> *Father, I desire that they also, whom You have given Me, be with Me where I am, so that they may see My glory which You have given Me, for You loved Me before the foundation of the world. Righteous Father, although the world has not known You, yet I have known You, and these have known that You sent Me; and I have made Your name known to them, and will make it known, so that the love with which You loved Me may be in them, and I in them.*
> (John 17:24–28 NASB)

They were united by a bond of LOVE that surpassed anything humans could understand or experience. Who knows for how long? For time held no meaning. They were totally and completely in full joy, peace, satisfaction, and delightful pleasure with being together, a beautiful, unbreakable bond, like a river surging back and forth from one to the other through the Holy Spirit.

God was fulfilled without creation. He did not need creation. The Triune council existed in perfect harmony, love, and joy. They needed nothing, lacked nothing, and desired nothing. Human words cannot describe the joy They shared. It was deep, abiding pleasure—all the time.

> *You will make known to me the way of life; In Your presence is fullness of joy; In Your right hand there are pleasures forever.* (Psalm 16:11 NASB)

All divine joy comes from God

Humans feel soulish emotions of happiness and physical contentment. We confuse joy with being *happy. Happiness* is an emotion; joy is a lifestyle. *Real joy is supernatural—divinely given.* It can only be had by the total giving of self for others. Occasionally, we get a taste of the overpowering euphoric satisfaction with life. Sometimes it is just looking at a sunset or watching a hummingbird or smelling fresh grass, and we are blessed with just a touch of pure divine joy and Shalom peace sweeping over us like a wave washing over the inner depths of both our soul and spirit. Only through God can we approach that divine experience of pure, 100 percent joy, for joy comes only when the soul and the spirit are in total harmony with one another, allowing the Holy Spirit to speak to us. True Joy is *Caught, not Taught.*

Think of the *most joyful time* in your life, when you held your newborn child in your arms for the first time, or when you said *"I do"* to the LOVE of your life. How you felt—euphoric, overwhelmed, your senses detached from your body while your mind and emotions floated on a canopy of seemingly endless happiness, content with everything and everyone, as waves of deep, satisfying love and gladness rolled across your entire being. It lasts for only a brief few seconds until, like a soft, gentle breeze, it moves on.

If you can sense that, feel that, experience that, then you have touched the very outer edge of that supernatural environment of unselfish LOVE, JOY, and PEACE that the Triune Godhead exists in.

The Holy Spirit *tosses* a "JOY PITCH" to our spirit, and we can *catch* a fleeting moment of the world of LOVE the Triune Godhead exist in. Why does He do that? We live in a fallen world, and true joy is not easily manifested, and when manifested, it is never kept for long. We cannot capture it, cannot claim it; we can only hold it for an instant before it is gone. He gives us a taste, a small sample, of what awaits us in eternity when we will dwell in the presence of God—joy, peace, complete fulfillment, and overwhelming contentment flooding our spirits forever.

If you love something, you want others to come and see it, feel it, know it, cherish it, and *love* it too. The Godhead existed in pure love and joy. Because God is good, He wanted to expand the universe with His goodness. Creation began with God's desire to magnify Himself and expand His goodness, love, and joy into all reaches of material reality. That was God's intent before creation, during creation, and since creation to this day. *His intent and purpose have not changed.*

Initially, we might think this to be a selfish or egotistical fault in God—to *expand* and *exalt* Himself. We think in those terms because we are human. God is not human. He does not think in those terms. His thoughts are far removed from our thoughts.

For humans, to expand ourselves outward, it is always at the expense of someone, some group, somewhere at some time. Man cannot be exalted except that someone must be de-exalted. Every *record* achieved is also a *record* broken. *Man* cannot advance without *overtaking* someone else. In a *fallen* world lacking LOVE and compassion, that soon develops fierce competition and carries pride, arrogance, condemnation, and self-centered promotion one against another.

God has no such restrictions. He has no such thoughts or feelings. There is no one above Him or beside Him. Expansion of His *glory* is at no one's expense. It is only an outward flow of love and goodness to share with His creation. There is no pride, no arrogance, no condemnation, for there is no one to be prideful or arrogant to. It is all about LOVE, AGAPE LOVE to share what is good. God is *good*, and He knows it is good to *expand* and *share* His goodness—and so He does. There is no competition; there is none above God to compete with.

A Plan to Share in His Glory

God is good. He knows no evil, holds no deceit, carries no grudges, nor entertains any thoughts of ill will. This is His GLORY—that *all His thoughts are* PURE, HOLY, *and can only produce* GOOD. In the great *council before the foundations of the world were laid,* the Triune Godhead decided to share this great GLORY, and so They created the universe and put a master plan together to create a voluntary family through whom They could share, reflect, and expand Their GLORY throughout all the material universe and beyond.

They did not have to—They wanted to.

In His LOVE, God gave us *free will* to make choices, even choices that went against His love and goodness. And so we did. We made poor choices, and we became outsiders, fatherless, homeless, and wandered aimlessly in creation in sin and failure. FATHER saw us, chose us, loved us, sought us out, and in his love for us, he put a plan together to rescue us. He sent His Son, Jesus, to be the perfect *diamond,* perfectly reflecting God's light to show us the way.

Divesting Himself of His GODLY attributes, Jesus—the Creator—became creation and lowered Himself to share Godhead's LOVE with creation.

> *He existed in the form of God, yet he gave no thought to seizing equality with God as his supreme prize. Instead he emptied himself of his outward glory by reducing himself to the form of a lowly servant. He became human! He humbled himself and became vulnerable, choosing to be revealed as a man and was obedient. He was a perfect example, even in his death—a criminal's death by crucifixion!* (Philippians 2:6–8 TPT)

Of all the reflections of light, the brightest is LOVE.

Scripture uses three analogies in describing believers of Jesus Christ. Each of these *correlates with a member of the Godhead,* and *each council member is expecting something from the decision made at the council meeting held before the foundations of the world were laid:*

- FATHER God sees us as *His children—His* Family, and He desires us to mature to receive an inheritance in the Kingdom. God desires a FAMILY of sons and daughters who are betrothed to His Beloved Son, Jesus, to become more like Christ in all ways.
- Jesus Messiah sees us as "His Bride," and He wants us to be adorned, arrayed, and spotless, worthy to receive HIM as *the* Groom, to co-rule and reign with Him in His Kingdom.
- HOLY SPIRIT sees us as His "tabernacle"—a dwelling place for *Him to reside within*—and He desires us to be HOLY and RIGHTEOUS before God. *The promise is that we will be priests after the order of Melchizedek, ministers to the God of creation, having free and open access to the Holy of Holies!*

Combined, the three viewpoints and desires of the Triune Godhead envelop the maturing process. In theological terms, we call this process *sanctification*. Each of these are fulfilled in the *fullness of God's plan*. This plan brings *glory* to God.

> *Therefore, when he had left, Jesus said, "Now is the Son of Man glorified, and God is glorified in Him; if God is glorified in Him, God will also glorify Him in Himself and will glorify Him immediately.* (John 13:31–32 NASB)

Defining Glory

The words *glory, gloried, glorified,* and *glorious* are used more than 540 times in the Creator's *Diary*. It is a lofty word and carries great significance to the magnificence of God.

In Hebrew, the word for *glory* is *ka'vowd*.[20] It means:

> *weighty, heavy in a good sense; honor, majesty, wealth.*

The Hebrew verb form of *glorify* is *ka'vad*.[21] And it means

> *to make weighty; to be made heavy in great honor; to multiply in a good way.*

Heavy in these tenses means

> *to increase the goodness and the power of.*

In the New Testament, the Greek form of the word is *dox'a*,[22] and it means

> *that which reflects or expresses or exhibits dignity honor.*

Strong's Concordance gives a theological definition as follows:

> *The celestial light which surrounds the celestial splendor in which God sits enthroned in divine effulgence, dazzling majesty, radiant glory; of internal character, glorious moral attributes, excellence, perfection, divine majesty, and holiness; the state of blissful perfection.*

---

[20] *The New Strong's Expanded Exhaustive Concordance of the Bible*, 2010, 126 OT.
[21] *The New Strong's Expanded Exhaustive Concordance of the Bible*, 2010, 125 OT.
[22] *The New Strong's Expanded Exhaustive Concordance of the Bible*, 2010, 71 NT.

The Greek verb form is *dox'azo*,[23] and it means

> *to honor; bestow honor on; to render honor*
> *praises, worship, and adoration. To exalt in dig-*
> *nity. To render excellent, splendid having the divine*
> *attributes and characteristics of God.*

In the Gospel of John, Jesus knew He was going to the cross, and HE prayed to the FATHER, not for Himself but for the FATHER to be *glorified*:

> *"Now My soul has become troubled; and what*
> *am I to say? 'Father, save Me from this hour'? But*
> *for this purpose, I came to this hour. Father, glo-*
> *rify Your name." Then a voice came out of heaven:*
> *"I have both glorified it and will glorify it again."*
> (John 12:27–28 NASB)

God audibly recognized and *glorified* His name.

Jesus gave us one of the most detailed and intimate glimpses into understanding the "glory of God'" when He faced the cross. His prayer, recorded in John's Gospel, chapter 17, referred to as the High Priestly Prayer, allows us to peek into the *most intimate corner of God's heart.*

> *Jesus spoke these things, and raising His eyes to*
> *heaven, He said, "Father, the hour has come; glorify*
> *Your Son, so that the Son may glorify You." (John*
> 17:1 NASB)

Jesus knows He is going to His death, the most dreadful death given within the Roman Empire—death by crucifixion. And His prayer to the Father is that the Father "glorify" Him! Why? So that Jesus may "glorify" the Father in His death. How does that happen?

---

[23] *The New Strong's Expanded Exhaustive Concordance of the Bible*, 2010, 72 NT.

How is the Father *glorified* by the brutal, humiliating death of His incarnate Son? And before you answer, look at this:

> *Though the Lord desired to crush him and make him ill.* (Isaiah 53:10 NASB)

God, the Father, "*desired*" to have His Son *crushed!* The usage here for the word *desired* means "*to be pleased.*" God is *pleased* to see HIS SON *crushed!*

This is the same Father who said, "*This is my beloved Son in whom I am well pleased.*" How can this same Father now say He is *pleased* to see His Son *crushed* by human torture? Sending His Son, whom He loved for eons before creation, to earth to be *crushed* on the cross is one thing, but to be *pleased* by doing so baffles the imagination. Why would the Father be *pleased* to "*crush*" His Son in such an evil and suffering manner? Is not God *love?*

Yes, He is LOVE, and it is because of *love* that He expresses HIS pleasure at seeing HIS SON crushed, love the Father has for you and me!

You see, God loves us as much as He loves His Son! That is LOVE we will never understand.

Let us look at the rest of that verse:

> *Though the Lord desired to crush him and make him ill, once restitution is made, he will see descendants and enjoy long life, and the Lord's purpose will be accomplished through him.* (Isaiah 53:10 NASB)

That is the GLORY OF THE LOVE the FATHER holds for each of us.

The Father holds each of us in the same loving regard that He holds Jesus. Before creation, before Adam, before we were ever a molecule, the FATHER loved us just as deeply, as dearly as He loved His Son, Yeshua, to the point of being pleased at sending Him to His torturous death so that we could share in their *glory*. Never will we understand such great LOVE.

And that is not all:

> *And this is eternal life, that they (us) may know*
> *You, the only true God, and Jesus Christ whom You*
> *have sent.* (John 17:3 NKJV)

Through this *crushing*, we are given the gift of *eternal life*, and not only *eternal life* but *eternal life knowing* God the Father as part of the Triune Godhead family!

> *I glorified You on the earth by accomplishing*
> *the work which You have given Me to do. And now*
> *You, Father, glorify Me together with Yourself, with*
> *the glory which I had with You before the world*
> *existed.* (Verses 4–5)

Doing the Father's WORK brought Jesus GLORY. He brought the LIGHT *of God to a dark world.* Our Mission is also to bring God GLORY. In turn, the Father *glorifies* the Son with the GLORY They held together "*before the world existed," and we will share in that glory.*

> *I have revealed Your name to the men whom*
> *You gave Me out of the world...they received...*
> *understood that I came forth from You, and they*
> *believed that You sent Me.* (Verses 6–8)

Before Jesus came, God was the great "I AM," a name so holy that it could not be pronounced on fear of death. Jesus showed us and gave us God's most intimate name—"Abba FATHER."

Glory is the visible, tangible manifestation of FATHERLOVE.

We are not only the *bride* of Christ, but we are the children of the FATHER. We are *kept* with *God's name* imprinted on our foreheads. We are *one* with the Father, just as Jesus is one with the Father.

> *I have given them Your word; and the world*
> *has hated them because they are not of the world,*

just as I am not of the world… Sanctify them in the truth. (Verses 14–17)

Once we receive and follow Jesus as Lord and Master, we are no longer citizens of this *Earth Age* but are citizens in the Kingdom of God—*"born again"* to be *"adopted"* of God.

> *I am not asking on behalf of these alone, but also for those who believe in Me through their word, that they may all be one; just as You, Father, are in Me and I in You, that they also may be in Us, so that the world may believe that You sent Me.* (Verses 18–21)

It did not end with the apostles. No. This tremendous outpouring of divine LOVE includes ALL who will receive the freely offered gift of love and inclusion. That includes you and me!

> *The glory which You have given Me I also have given to them, so that they may be one, just as We are one; I in them and You in Me, that they may be perfected in unity, so that the world may know that You sent Me, and You loved them, just as You loved Me.* (Verses 22–24)

Let us never look at this transformation as a progression or some *lower* form of love to a *higher* form of love. As we progress in our sanctification, God's love for us never changes. He cannot love us any more than He does, and His love never falters, pauses, or decreases. We will always be His *children*, and we get to *know* God, to *know* our Father—"Abba Father"—intimately, *face-to-face* fellowship with the Triune Godhead. The *love* that God lavished on His Son, *He lavishes on us. He gives us life—and more abundantly!*—not the *things* of this temporal world but the things that the earthly world does not have, things which are beyond price, beyond value and worth, and which the world does not and cannot possess. We mature to be coheirs with

Christ in the Kingdom of God! Recall God's promise at the end of the *Diary*:

> *And He said to me, "It is done! I am the Alpha and the Omega, the Beginning, and the End. I will give of the fountain of the water of life freely to him who thirsts. He who overcomes shall inherit all things, and I will be his God, and he shall be My son (huios)."* (Revelation 21:6–7 NKJV)

God's PLAN is for us to become *coheirs with Christ of the Kingdom of God to share in His* GLORY.

The Inheritance

We may wonder what exactly is the *inheritance* God is giving us as coheirs with Christ in the Kingdom. Jesus answered that question for us.

Approximately thirty years after Nero beheaded the Apostle Paul, a new emperor was in place by the name of Domitian. At that time, the only remaining apostle of the original twelve was John, who headed the movement from Ephesus. He was arrested and dragged off to Rome. He was over ninety years old at the time. Church tradition claims that Domitian had John thrown into a vat of boiling oil and that John climbed out unscathed. This so *unnerved* the emperor that he went into a rant and had John exiled to the Isle of Patmos, which was a *prison of no return*. While there, the Lord came to John and showed him a *revelation* which John recorded and is the final book of the *Diary*—"*The Revelation of Jesus Christ.*"

At the beginning of the Revelation, the Lord stands amid seven lampstands representing seven *Ekklesias* of Asia Minor. Among other interpretations, the seven *Ekklesias* represent different stages the *church* can find itself in. Jesus gives John seven letters, one for each *Ekklesia*. Each letter includes the following:

- First, what pitfalls that *Ekklesia* needs to overcome in its walk with Christ.

- Second, what undesirable result will follow if these pitfalls are not *overcome*.
- Third, what *reward* God is offering to them if these pitfalls are *overcome*.

This is a *Kingdom* message, and when summed together, these *rewards* define the kingdom *"inheritance."* The following chart lists each *Ekklesia* location (along with the Scripture), what pitfall they need to overcome, what will happen if they do not overcome the pitfall, and what reward they will *inherit* if they do overcome the pitfall.

Location (Scripture)	Pitfall to Overcome	Reward Inheritance
Ephesus (2:1)	*loss* of first love	Tree of Life, Bride of Christ, Glorified bodies, Partakers of *Glory*
Smyrna (2:9)	persecution	Crown of life, coreign with Christ, no *second* death, eternal life Godhead
Pergamum (2:12)	false teaching	Hidden manna, Intimacy and Holiness, White stone name, Honor as His sons
Thyatira (2:18)	spirit of Jezebel	Authority to rule, Morning star
Sardis (3:1)	staying alert	Wedding garments for the Marriage of the Lamb, Book of Life, Kingdom citizenship
Philadelphia (3:7)	remain faithful	Pillar in the Temple of Priesthood in the Kingdom
Laodicea (3:14)	lukewarm	Sit with Christ on His throne, Fellowship and reigning with Christ for eternity

Eternal life, hidden stone, manna from heaven, a new name, new clothes, a priestly place in the temple, authority to rule with Christ, name in the Book of Life, and to sit with Christ on the throne—all promises of the Kingdom inheritance!

There is much emphasis on these promises of receiving a new name, a name that covers many blessings. In Scripture, names are meaningful, and God gives new names to show His purpose and pleasure with the person (i.e., Abraham and Jacob). As "*coheirs*" with Christ in the Kingdom, being "*born again*" and "*adopted*," we are rewarded with a multifaceted new name, giving us a new identity in the Kingdom. That identity comes equipped with the authority to rule the nations and peoples of the world. Even greater glory is that we are invited to "*sit on the throne*" along with our Lord. Who would have ever thought we would be given such honor—such *glory*—with which to honor and *glorify* the FATHER? Let us look at the promises of a new name:

- First, "*I will give him a white stone and on the stone a new name written, which no one knows except he who receives it.*" Each *overcomer* is given a personal new name, in secret, that only each of us and God knows. It is a name that reflects who we are in the Kingdom and how our life reflected Christ.
- Second, "*I will write on him the name of My God and the name of the city of My God, the New Jerusalem, which comes down out of heaven from My God.*" We are given the name of the FATHER and the *city* of the FATHER. This is akin to the *adoption* process, where the *mature son* receives the *father's* name and heritage. We are marked with FATHERLOVE's name, declaring we are of His family—He is our FATHER.
- Third, "*And My own new name.*" We are given the name of Jesus as His "bride." We are united with Christ and go forth as His *Ekklesia*—His body, His church—coheirs alongside the King to rule, reign, and worship in the Kingdom.

Further, we are given new white garments, our formal dining clothing for the *"marriage supper of the lamb."* We are invited to partake of the *"hidden manna"* and be *"pillars in the temple of God,"* which is to have a "Holy of Holies" intimate relationship with the FATHER. The *"hidden manna"* was the manifestation of God's presence and was kept in the Ark of the Covenant located inside the "Most Holy Place"—the *Holy of Holies*. The veil has been torn asunder, and as *overcomers*, we are invited to partake of God's most Holy Presence. We are given crowns and invited to sit on the throne, reigning with Christ. Just allow the thought to sink in and take hold of your spirit. Such unimaginable GLORY given to us as free gifts from our LOVING FATHER!

Summarizing these rewards reveals a clear picture of the LOVE the FATHER holds for His sons and daughters. Taking us in stages from *"glory to glory." Rolled together, we are promised eternal, intimate fellowship and rulership and ministry with the Triune Godhead,* an eternity of being part of God's family! Remain faithful to your calling. Do not become complacent, lukewarm, deceived, or allow your focus to drift from the *person* of Jesus to the *things* of Jesus. We are promised an eternity of intimate fellowship and rulership with God. Just think, we can fellowship with God—face-to-face—and not be consumed, something even Moses could not do. Oh, the glories! No wonder Paul could not contain himself when he was shown such wonders!

When we think about what God has in store for us, it causes us to gush forth, overflowing with indescribable joy to where we cannot contain ourselves! Beginning here on earth, in this present *Earth Age* with the Holy Spirit indwelling in our spirits, continuing into the Kingdom Age, and then outward into all of eternity, God has made a plan where He invites us to journey with Him. How can we not sing in the midst of persecution?

Earth Age Glory

We can take all the cares, worries, and fears of this age and discard them as so much meaningless clutter and replace them with the overwhelming solace of God in our souls. What pure joy! What divine rest and peace the world does not and can never know. It can only come by knowing the FATHER, and Jesus opened the door to us, revealing the FATHER to us and inviting us in to know Him as He knew Him. God's magnificence, purity, truth, and holiness—His *glory*—infused into us to be reflected out into a dark world, packaged in love and goodness, sent out to bring life and light. That is the beginning of moving from glory to glory.

And it is only the beginning.

> *I have come that they may have life and that they may have it more abundantly.* (John 10:10 NKJV)

Receiving Jesus gives us His life inside of us "*more abundantly.*" It is not about prosperity, having the newest car, or a fat bank account. If you have those things, good; use them for the glory of God! But having life "*more abundantly*" with Christ is not about those things. It is about having more of Him—more of His love, more of His grace, more of HIM "*more abundantly*"—living within us and reflecting out into the world. It is having "*more abundantly*" the true gifts and *fruit* of the Spirit we can only get from HIM.

Inner peace—overwhelming joy in the face of hardship and persecution—the *trusted hope* of a future of *eternal bliss and purpose* with the Triune Godhead, having the *fullness* of *His stature* inside of us, *overflowing with His love and truth*, the very things that make all the riches of this world pale into insignificance, that is the GLORY of being His *son and daughter* in this *Earth Age*.

The GLORY of the FATHER is that we do not have to wait until we pass from this *Earth Age* to enjoy the "fullness of His stature." God has provided for us, here and now, to experience the first level of GLORY upon our receiving of Jesus as our Lord and Savior. The Holy Spirit takes up residence in our spirits and begins the *maturing* process to transform us into the living images of Christ. We become new creatures, having God breathing and living inside of us! As limited as we are, living in these *earth suits,* we are enabled to experience the first level of the GLORY of God in our spirits and souls. It is by the supernatural spiritual awakening of "Caught, not Taught" that the Holy Spirit matures us to be equipped with the Power of LOVE to go forth into the harvest of these *end* times. *We enjoy the fruits of a holy life, free from the chains of earth.*

Kingdom Age Glory

God's Ultimate Purpose and Plan will be realized, and the *harmony of the Garden* will be restored to the world once again. This will be accomplished during the Kingdom Age.

> *The eager expectation of the creation waits for the appearance of the sons of God...that creation itself also will be set free from its slavery to corruption into the glorious freedom of the children of God... We know that the whole creation groans and travails in pain together until now. Not only that, but we also, who have the first fruits of the Spirit, groan within ourselves while eagerly waiting for adoption, the redemption of our bodies.* (Romans 8:18–23 NASB)

It will happen after the world has completely gone insane with evil and darkness, that God will release His PLAN for the *Kingdom Age.* The world will be on the brink of total annihilation and destruction, in total despair, having no hope, no peace, no understanding. Only suffering, pain, hopelessness, and death surround it and lacking any promise of a future. At this point, the lowest point in all of creation's history, is when the Son of the Living God will return to earth to claim His Kingdom!

Entering the *Kingdom Age*, also known as the Millennial Age, we will rule and reign alongside the King of kings over all the nations of the earth as priests after the order of Melchizedek, priest/kings worshipping, ministering, serving God. What a privilege we are given to share and expand His *glory* throughout the world.

Creation was made for Christ to be the centerpiece, and when He takes His place, among all the world's kingdoms, there will be a rebirth of all aspects of creation into a fullness of glory unheard of or unseen ever before. God's original intent with the Garden of Eden will be realized. Just think, every tree, every blade of grass, every living creature, every rainbow is bursting with anticipation to come forth in their purest form of expression for life and joy at being created! Colors, sounds, freedom from want, from fear, from futility all to overflow with life. *The Garden of Eden expanded across the entire globe.*

And His bride will come with Him to "*inherit*" the Kingdom of Heaven on earth, to ride out of those clouds alongside Paul and John and Peter, alongside Jesus, the Messiah! What joy! Bringing God's plan to fulfillment since *before the foundations of the world were laid!* What a glorious, unforgettable day that will be! To bring and establish the GLORY of FATHERLOVE to His creation! What an honor! What joy! To be chosen by God! Undeserved, unmerited, only by the sheer gift of grace from FATHERLOVE, spreading the *glory* of God and expanding His goodness.

Just think of all the beautiful things you have experienced at one time or another in your life—the *joy* of family, the fragrant flowers, the soft summer breeze, the deep blue sky, and the ocean's surf. Think of the joy that flowed through you and filled you with passion and happiness. And think of a world that is nothing but all those things—for all times—having no evil, no pain, no heartache, no suffering, no discord, fighting, jealousy, or hatred. All races and people at peace with one another emerged in the light of FATHERLOVE. A world of light, love, and truth completely engulfed in holiness and purity, creation as the Godhead originally intended during that council meeting *before the foundations of the world were laid,* finally, the world as it was designed to be—the Garden of Eden.

It is the marriage of the Begotten Son of God to the Ekklesia in God's Ultimate Plan. Everything leads to this marriage culminated in the great wedding supper described in the Apostle John's revelation on the Isle of Patmos:

> *Then I heard something like the sound like a*
> *great multitude, as the sound of many waters and as*

the sound of mighty thundering, saying: "Alleluia! For the Lord God Omnipotent reigns! Let us be glad and rejoice and give Him glory, for the marriage of the Lamb has come, and His wife has made herself ready. It was granted her to be arrayed in fine linen, clean and white." Fine linen is the righteous deeds of the saints. Then he said to me, "Write: Blessed are those who are invited to the marriage supper of the Lamb." (Revelation 19:6–8 MEV)

Let us look at Romans 8:19–22 again, this time from *The Passion Translation*:

> *The entire universe is standing on tiptoe, yearning to see the unveiling of God's glorious sons and daughters! For against its will, the universe itself has had to endure the empty futility resulting from the consequences of human sin. But now, with eager expectation, all creation longs for freedom from its slavery to decay and to experience with us the wonderful freedom coming to God's children. To this day, we are aware of the universal agony and groaning of creation, as if it were in the contractions of labor for childbirth. (Romans 8:19–22 TPT)*

As the Kingdom Age advances, the Millennium Era of a thousand years will proceed. Satan will be removed from the earth. Jesus Christ will reign from Jerusalem, and all the nations will come to worship.

> *At that time, they will call Jerusalem, the Throne of the Lord, and all the nations will be gathered to it, to Jerusalem, for the name of the Lord; nor will they walk any more after the stubbornness of their evil hearts. (Jeremiah 3:17 MEV)*

> *Then it will be that all the nations who have come against Jerusalem and survived will go up each year to worship the King, the Lord of Hosts, and to celebrate the Feast of Tabernacles.* (Zechariah 14:16 MEV)

Many of God's children will grow and mature into adopted sons of God during this time, and there will be the greatest harvest ever witnessed in history.

> *But we all, with unveiled faces, looking as in a mirror at the glory of the Lord, are being transformed into the same image from glory to glory, just as from the Lord, the Spirit.* (2 Corinthians 3:18 NASB)

> *Arise, shine; for your light has come, And the glory of the Lord has risen upon you. For behold, darkness will cover the earth, and deep darkness the peoples; But the Lord will rise upon you, And His glory will appear upon you.* (Isaiah 60:1–2 NASB)

Next to the cross itself, this age of *glory* is the greatest demonstration of Fatherlove, as the Father will give millions the opportunity to find and know His Son, Jesus Christ, and find eternal salvation.[24]

The Eternal Age Glory

And that is still not all, far from it. Those *ages* are just the bare beginnings. Following the Millennium, we reflect God's pure light and love into all the universe as we go forth to expand, share, and spread the great love of the FATHER, to share all His glory and greatness, to allow us to reflect all His breathtaking glory into the universe expanding forever and ever!

---

[24] See Appendix B for a discussion on the Millennium.

Of the increase of his government and peace there shall be no end, upon the throne of David and over his kingdom, to order it and to establish it with justice and with righteousness, from now until forever. (Isaiah 9:7 MEV)

To rule and reign with Him for all eternity! To receive unmerited *favor and glory* from the Triune Godhead! To have intimacy with God on a one-on-one, face-to-face basis! To carry God's name, His LIFE, LOVE, and SPIRIT, for ALL ETERNITY! Those are the rewards! That is the inheritance we are freely, undeservedly, and lovingly given. How is it possible we can be so blessed?

A new heaven and a new earth will be birthed.

Then I saw a new heaven and a new earth; for the first heaven and the first earth passed away, there is no longer any sea. And I saw the holy city, new Jerusalem, coming down out of heaven from God, prepared as a bride adorned for her husband. And I heard a loud voice from the throne, saying, "Behold, the tabernacle of God is among the people, and He will dwell among them, and they shall be His people, and God Himself will be among them, and He will wipe away every tear from their eyes; and there will no longer be any death; there will no longer be any mourning, or crying, or pain; the first things have passed away." (Revelation 21:1–4 NASB)

No longer will you have the sun for light by day, nor will the moon give you light for brightness; But you will have the Lord as an everlasting light, And your God as your glory. Your sun will no longer set, nor will your moon wane; For you will have the Lord as an everlasting light, And the days of your mourning will be over. (Isaiah 60:19–20 NASB)

And the city has no need of the sun or of the moon to shine on it, for the glory of God has illuminated it, and its lamp is the Lamb. (Revelation 21:23 NASB)

The one who overcomes will inherit these things, and I will be his God, and he will be My son. (Revelation 21:7 NASB)

And you can be a part of it.

This love is not only for something to dream about or wish over. No, it is also for you, reader. God desires that you share in this glory, that you are given a white horse to ride, a new name, a white set of garments, access to the hidden manna, a crown, a morning star, and coheir with Jesus Christ in the kingdom of God. This is not a fairy tale you read about and then sigh in despair thinking, *Oh, if only…"* No, this is real, and most importantly, this can be your story as well. All you need to do is say YES to Jesus. *"YES, I receive you as my Lord, Savior, and will serve alongside You in the glorious Kingdom of God."*

Become a "son or daughter" of the Most High God, the King who did it all for you. What decision in your entire life could even come close to the decision to LIVE in JOY, PEACE, and LOVE with the Creator of all things?

APPENDIX A

THE UNVEILING—2

For thousands of years, man wondered about the world around him. What was it? Where did it come from? How did it get here? What was God's *Ultimate Purpose* with creation? What was His PLAN? Or was it all just random, just happened to be here with no real purpose or plan?

We have come a long way on our quest to find that answer, and we have seen, from the *Diary,* that there is a *Purpose* and a *Plan*—God's *Purpose* and *Plan*. Two thousand years ago, God took the Apostle Paul on a *helicopter* ride and showed him the *"hidden mystery"* of God's *secret plan,* who then revealed it to the world:

> *And through the revelation of the Anointed One, he unveiled his secret desires to us—the hidden mystery of his long-range plan, which he was delighted to implement from the very beginning of time.* (Ephesians 1:9 TPT)

The First Unveiling

Paul expounded on this revelation throughout his Letters to the *Ekklesia* he had established. Along with *"Christ and Him crucified,"* it became the central theme of his preaching from that time onward. In his universal Letter to the Ephesians, Paul revealed God's desire to have a "family" of "adopted" sons to further *expand* His GLORY and LOVE throughout the universe, through His *Beloved Son*, Jesus Christ:

> *He made known to us the mystery of His will,*
> *according to His kind intention which He purposed*
> *in Him.* (Ephesians 1:9 NASB)

> *To bring to light what is the administration of*
> *the mystery which for ages has been hidden in God*
> *who created all things... This was in accordance*
> *with the eternal purpose which He carried out in*
> *Christ Jesus our Lord.* (Ephesians 3:9, 11 NASB)

In his letter to the Colossians, Paul showed Jesus as the "centerpiece" of the *secret plan*. All would flow *by, from, to, for*, and *through* Him. The "inherited" sons would receive their *co-inheritance* by their acceptance of Jesus Messiah as Savior, Lord, and Master:

> *He is also head of the body, the church; and He*
> *is the beginning, the firstborn from the dead so that*
> *He Himself will come to have first place in every-*
> *thing. For it was the Father's good pleasure for all*
> *the fullness to dwell in Him, and through Him to*
> *reconcile all things to Himself, having made peace*
> *through the blood of His cross...that is, the mystery*
> *which has been hidden from the past ages and gen-*
> *erations, but has now been manifested to His saints,*
> *to whom God willed to make known what is the*
> *riches of the glory of this mystery...which is Christ*
> *in you, the hope of glory.* (Colossians 1:18–20,
> 27–28 NASB)

In all his letters to the believers in the churches throughout the Roman Empire, Paul expounded on God's *Original Plan* to have a "family," and he repeatedly encouraged and instructed believers on *maturing* as coheirs of the Kingdom with Christ:

> *For all who are being led by the Spirit of God, these are sons of God...but you have received a spirit of adoption as sons... The Spirit Himself testifies with our spirit that we are children of God, and if children, heirs also, heirs of God and fellow heirs with Christ, if indeed we suffer with Him so that we may also be glorified with Him...waiting eagerly for our adoption as sons.* (Romans 8:14–25 NASB)

> *But we all...are being transformed into the same image from glory to glory.* (2 Corinthians 3:18 NASB)

> *But when the fullness of the time came, God sent forth His Son...that we might receive the adoption as sons... Therefore you are no longer a slave, but a son; and if a son, then an heir through God.* (Galatians 4:4–7 NASB)

This was a glorious revelation given to the Apostle Paul, and we thank our Lord for this "unveiling" of His *secret plan* to him.

Looking for Confirmation

Despite this wonderful revelation and news, we cannot help but wonder, was this revelation only revealed to Paul, and as such, do we have only a single witness to stand upon? Does not Scripture teach that there should be two witnesses to truth?

> *Even in your Law it has been written that the testimony of two people is true. I am He who testifies about Myself, and the Father who sent Me testifies about Me.* (John 8:17–18 NASB)

Yes, we have *confirmation* of God's *Purpose*, by our Lord Himself, with His references to the *kingdom'* and the believers' inheritance, but that does not go into the detail that Paul did. Is that enough? We know there were confusion and misunderstanding about the *kingdom* among the Apostles who were looking for a *worldly* kingdom, overcoming the Roman Empire, so one would think it would have been made more concrete and clear.

There are also various *promises, prophecies,* and *quotations* from the Tanakh's prophets (Hebrew Bible), which can be interpreted to apply to God's *Original Purpose,* and these are important and good. But we still cannot help but think the "unveiling" of God's *Purpose,* which was "hidden" for millenniums, would warrant more than a single witness. Even Jesus was given a *human* witness of testimony:

> *If I alone testify about Myself, My testimony is not true. There is another who testifies about Me, and I know that the testimony which He gives about Me is true. You have sent messengers to John, and he has testified to the truth.* (John 5:31–33 NASB)

> *A man came, one sent from God, and his name was John. He came as a witness, to testify about the Light, so that all might believe through him. He was not the Light, but he came to testify about the Light.* (John 1:6–8 NKJV)

The "unveiling" of God's *Original Purpose and Plan* with creation is of such magnitude and importance that we would expect a clear and decisive witness to Paul's words. Already, even in Paul's day, many "false doctrines" were springing up about Christ and the Gospel. Many false teachers and groups, such as *legalistic Jewish rabbis* and the *Gnostics,* were rising, teaching perverted falsehoods and doctrines. And today, generations removed from Paul, thousands of denominations and doctrines exist, arguing and fighting over the smallest, trivial of things. So should there not be confirmation of Paul's "out of body experience" in the *Diary* to verify that this is not just one more?

In addition, consider that Paul himself was "suspect." He was not one of the twelve apostles who had lived and followed Jesus but, rather, was the number one "persecutor" of the church, overseeing the murder of Stephen. As such, his conversion was held by many in suspicion and mistrust. It took many years for most to "accept" him as sincere and legitimate into the movement (perhaps that is why he did not speak about his *out-of-body* experience until fourteen years afterward). Even then, they had problems accepting and understanding his doctrines.

> *Even as our beloved brother Paul has also written to you according to the wisdom given to him. As in all his letters, he writes about these things, in which some things are hard to understand, which the unlearned and unstable distort, as they also do the other Scriptures, to their own destruction.* (2 Peter 3:15–16 MEV)

We can visualize people asking, "*Why would God reveal such an important mystery to Paul—the persecutor? Why not to Peter the Rock, or to John the Beloved? Why not unveil it to James, the brother of Jesus and head of the church in Jerusalem?*"

We wonder if the apostles themselves did not murmur and grumble about Paul getting these revelations they had not received? And we wonder how they would receive such an important revelation from *Paul*, the *persecutor*.

How do the followers of Christ, then and now, know that this revelation is indeed *God sent* and is not a *doctrine* devised by Paul to put himself above or set himself apart from the original twelve?

One obstacle to having a second witness to confirm this revelation is the timing. Paul did not receive the revelation of the "*mystery unveiled*" until a decade after Jesus walked the earth. What kind of confirmation or witness would convince the church that it was real that long after Jesus had departed?

Also, one would think that either the initial "unveiling" itself or a "witness" to the "unveiling" would come from within the group of twelve apostles who had traveled and lived with Jesus on earth. They are the ones whom Jesus had groomed to carry out the *Great Commission* and looked up to as the authorities. And they were quickly dying off. Within a couple of decades, there was only one remaining.

Without *confirmation,* this critical "unveiling" runs the risk of being lost, discarded, or minimized to a minor facet or a distorted doctrine of Christianity.

But God…would not allow that to happen. It was too important. There would be a *second witness.*

The Second Unveiling

The Apostle John underwent persecution and was banished into exile by Emperor Domitian[25] onto the remote Isle of Patmos[26] around thirty years after Nero executed Paul. He was the last of the original Apostles remaining.

During his exile, John also had an *out-of-body* experience. The Lord Himself came to John and gave him a *deluxe helicopter ride* covering the entire length of God's "parade" route!

Over the generations, there have been many interpretations, discourse, arguments, and scenarios attempting to *interpret* John's experience as it consists of many images, symbols, and visions regarding its apocalyptic message. We can think of all those images and visions as being like those gigantic balloons floating above Macy's Thanksgiving Parade. From the *helicopter* view, they bounce and float around and obstruct the view of the parade below. More volumes have been written, and a constant stream of theories have sprung up regarding this final *chapter* of God's *Diary* than any other *chapter.*

It is not our intent to add any additional *ingredients* to this boiling cauldron of interpretations, theories, movies, and doctrines. We are taking a different look at this book in the *Diary.* So just for a moment, let us set aside all the symbols and images, leaving them

---

[25] https://en.wikipedia.org/wiki/Domitian.

[26] https://en.wikipedia.org/wiki/John_of_Patmos.

for the *experts* to interpret and look at the overall message and flow of John's vision and supernatural experience. In other words, let's remove all those gigantic balloons floating above and obstructing the view below and focus on the parade itself.

When we do this, it becomes clear that one of the reasons for John's out-of-body experience is to be a *witness and confirmation* to Paul's "unveiling" of God's "mystery"!

The opening verse sets the tone of the message:

> *The Revelation of Jesus Christ, which God gave*
> *Him to show to His bond-servants, the things which*
> *must soon take place.* (Revelation 1:1 NASB)

We have seen that God's *plan* resided totally *in, by, for, with, and through* Jesus Messiah. What John is being shown is not the *revelation of end-time events* but is the "Revelation of Jesus" pertaining to the "things which must take place." On the cross, Jesus said, *"It is finished,"* and the only thing we're waiting for that "must take place" is the final phase of God's *plan* to fully install the Kingdom to earth, which consists of Jesus returning as the "head" of the church to collect His bride and grant "coheirship" to the "mature sons of God' in the Kingdom. Look at this declaration from Revelation:

> *And He who sits on the throne said, "Behold,*
> *I am making all things new." And He said, "Write,*
> *for these words are faithful and true." Then He said*
> *to me, "It is done. I am the Alpha and the Omega,*
> *the beginning and the end. I will give to the one*
> *who thirsts from the spring of the water of life with-*
> *out cost. He who overcomes will inherit these things,*
> *and I will be his God, and he will be My son."*
> (Revelation 21:5–7 NASB)

To be an *overcomer* requires growth, testing, and maturity.

Paul's ministry ended with Paul in prison sending letters to his churches encouraging the *Ekklesia* to grow into "maturity" as *over-*

comers to be adopted as "coheirs" with Christ in the Kingdom of God. We saw that even Paul himself was waiting for the final reward of becoming an "*adopted son.*"

John's vision *picks up where Paul's ministry left off*, with Jesus standing in the midst of His *Ekklesia*, encouraging the believers to be *overcomers* (mature sons), so they can "*inherit*" the Kingdom.

Jesus gives John seven letters—one for each of the seven churches He stands with. These churches represent the various stages and situations the body of Christ has found itself faced with and still does today. As reviewed in chapter 11, "The Ekklesia," the letters offer instruction, correction, and admonishment for shortcomings. But each encourages believers to be overcomers, offering Kingdom rewards:

> *To the one who overcomes, I will grant to eat from the tree of life, which is in the Paradise of God.* (Revelation 2:7 NASB)

> *The one who overcomes will not be hurt by the second death.* (Revelation 2:11 NASB)

> *To the one who overcomes, I will give some of the hidden manna, and I will give him a white stone, and a new name written on the stone which no one knows except the one who receives it.* (Revelation 2:17 NASB)

> *The one who overcomes, and the one who keeps My deeds until the end, I will give him authority over the nations; and he shall rule them with a rod of iron...and I will give him the morning star.* (Revelation 2:26–28 NASB)

> *The one who overcomes will be clothed the same way, in white garments; and I will not erase his name from the book of life, and I will confess*

his name before My Father and before His angels.
(Revelation 3:5 NASB)

> *The one who overcomes, I will make him a*
> *pillar in the temple of My God, and he will not*
> *go out from it anymore; and I will write on him*
> *the name of My God, and the name of the city of*
> *My God, the new Jerusalem, which comes down*
> *out of heaven from My God, and My new name.*
> (Revelation 3:12 NASB)

> *The one who overcomes, I will grant to him*
> *to sit with Me on My throne, as I also overcame*
> *and sat with My Father on His throne.* (Revelation
> 3:21 NASB)

Every one of these *promises* to the *overcomers* is a *Kingdom* promise in complete agreement with the promises made in Paul's Letters to the *Ekklesia,* and with the promises Jesus made to His *believers* while on earth.

Altogether, they can be summed up as follows: *He who overcomes will be adopted as a coheir son of God in the Kingdom of God.*

Can anything be more transparent?

The "Revelation of Jesus Christ" also begins with a special blessing:

> *Blessed is he who reads and those who hear the*
> *words of the prophecy and heed the things which are*
> *written in it; for the time is near.* (Revelation 1:3
> NASB)

Why is there a special *blessing* given to those who *read and heed* this "*revelation*"?

Because this message comes directly from Jesus to His church and confirms the eternal *plan* of the godly *council.* Those who "*heed*" will become the "*coheirs*" with Christ in the Kingdom.

The "*Revelation of Jesus Christ*" ends with a special promise:

> *And He said to me, "Do not seal up the words
> of the prophecy of this book, for the time is near...
> Behold, I am coming quickly, and My reward is
> with Me, to render to every man according to what
> he has done. I am the Alpha and the Omega, the
> first and the last, the beginning and the end. Blessed
> are those who wash their robes, so that they may
> have the right to the tree of life, and may enter
> by the gates into the city... I, Jesus, have sent My
> angel to testify to you these things for the churches."*
> (Revelation 22:10, 12–17 NASB)

John wrote down the details of his experience, and it closes out God's *Diary as confirmation of God's Ultimate Purpose and Plan.*

And in God's divine providence and wisdom, it is given to the last living of the original twelve apostles (for credibility) by Jesus Himself (for authority and finality)!

The Book of Revelation includes great prophecies regarding the *end times,* but setting aside all the symbolism, it also confirms God's *Ultimate Purpose and Plan* with creation.

The vision begins with Jesus presenting Himself to John. John had spent three and a half years living with Jesus. He was the disciple who *leaned on Jesus's breast,* the disciple that "*Jesus loved.*" One would expect John to easily recognize Jesus when he sees Him. Yet he does not! This is not the same Jesus John knew! This is not the Jesus who was birthed in a manger, who died on a cross, or even the Jesus who rose from the tomb and whom John had watched ascend into heaven! No, this is the victorious, conquering King of kings, the "*Beloved*" Son of God, who now resides with the Father and has all authority in heaven and earth and holds the keys to death and hell. He is arrayed in His splendor and glory! His countenance is again as unapproachable light, and John falls to his feet in awe, wonder, and worship.

> *Then I turned to see the voice that was speaking with me... I saw one like a son of man, clothed in a robe reaching to the feet, and girded across His chest with a golden sash. His head and His hair were white like white wool, like snow; and His eyes were like a flame of fire. His feet were like burnished bronze, when it has been made to glow in a furnace, and His voice was like the sound of many waters. In His right hand He held seven stars, and out of His mouth came a sharp two-edged sword; and His face was like the sun shining in its strength.* (Revelation 1:12–16 NASB)

Yes, there is a large array of apocalyptic events that unfold and are highlighted throughout the vision. We do not claim to understand them or to have *revelatory* insight to interpret them. That part of the *Diary* is not pertinent to this message. That will all play out as God ordains it to. He alone rides in His *helicopter* high overhead and sees the *beginning from the end*. He is the "*Alpha and the Omega*." He is in charge, and all will occur as He decrees.

However, those events will finally play out. We know that they will all work together to bring closure to God's *Original Plan* of creation, bringing the *kingdom of heaven on earth*, co-inherited by a family of "sons and daughters" through Jesus Christ, to *extend God's love and glory* throughout all of creation.

When we read the last "chapter" of God's *Diary*—"*The Revelation of Jesus Christ*"—through the lens of God's *Ultimate Intention, Purpose, and Plan*, we do not need to get hung up on attempting to interpret various symbols and events. We only rejoice in seeing total *confirmation* of God's PLAN for creation and humankind. *Revelation* is the last remaining phase of the PLAN with Christ returning to collect His bride (*the church*), along with the long-awaited, highly anticipated corporate "*adoption*" graduation ceremony into the family of God as "coheirs" with Christ, followed by the great *wedding* feast celebration and the establishment of the Kingdom of heaven on earth, bringing the New Jerusalem to earth and the reign with our Lord for eternity, throughout the universe.

To Him be the glory, forever and ever!

Yes, the *Ultimate Purpose* of God's creating the universe is *unveiled a second time*, witnessed and confirmed.

We thank God for His "unveiling" of the "mystery," both to the Apostle Paul and then to the Apostle John, for it gives us an understanding of our purpose while we are on this side of the journey. And we know, no matter what happens in the future, no matter what all those *symbols* and *events* (all those floating balloons) will end up looking like, we can live in peace, "*anxious for nothing,*" because we read the *Diary*, and we know how the story ends: *We reign forever with our Lord, Savior, and King in the new heaven and earth.*

Thank you, Father, for being such a good Father. You truly are Fatherlove.

APPENDIX B

OUR STORY

In the late fall of 2019, we were talking about a statement from Dr. Harold Eberle's book *Systematic Theology for the New Apostolic Reformation*:

> *God started as a loving Father determined to have sons, and He will finish as a loving Father with sons.*

We commented that Harold had placed that statement at both the beginning and at the end of his book! It obviously held great meaning for him, and we were caught by the powerful impact, influence, and impartation of the concepts and principles hidden in that statement. As a result, we began having some *breakfast* meetings to discuss and bounce different ideas off one another. The focus of our discussions and questions seemed to center around "*Why did God do Creation? What was His Purpose and Intention?*"

The one thing we enjoy most together is sharing the joy and pleasure we receive when God is GLORIFIED through our lives! Our *breakfast* meetings became the highlight of our week as we could not wait to unveil the latest *revelation* in our quest for answers to our questions.

As those discussions continued and began going a little deeper into Scripture, we both were separately challenged by the Holy Spirit to coauthor the book you are holding: *Created by Love—Created to Love, Like Father—Like Sons.*

Let us introduce ourselves.

We are

- *Paul Bersche*. In ministry for sixty-four years, a church *planter* and pastor-teacher, focused on being a living expression of the lifestyle we promote in this book. I am eighty-four years old and married to my marvelous wife, Carolyn, for over sixty plus years.
- *Duane Levick*. A Messianic Jew, retired businessman. Called to *teach* and write the Word of God. An author and teacher. I am seventy-four years young.

So one could say, we are two old soldiers with some number of years of experience in knowing and walking with the FATHER. We love the Word of God and anticipate with great joy the thrill of discussing spiritual revelation our FATHER lovingly shares with us and passing it on to the younger generations in the *Ekklesia*!

Coauthoring a book is not as easy as it may sound. When we began writing together, we still were in the beginning stages of the process of proving our relationship with each other. As time progressed, we were confident the FATHER had placed us together for this purpose and that we needed to work hard to give Him an acceptable and worthy product. But we knew there would be some challenges. Little did we know how big they would be! Our major concern was being on the same wavelength in our thinking and reasoning.

As things unfolded, our working relationship was the simplest part of all to hurdle. The Holy Spirit communicated between our spirits, and we were always in perfect sync together, even when the direction and focus on the book's content shifted during the writing.

We developed the strategy for putting together the ideas for topics and chapters, discussing every weekend, and then reading, correcting, proofing, and discussing what had been written the previous week. Our motto became *"Converse...Write...Review...Repeat."*

We had established a comfortable pattern when our world turned upside down. On the last weekend of January 2020, the president of the United States shut down air traffic with China and other popular travel nations worldwide.

The COVID-19 pandemic had hit…hard…and changed our lives.

Governors became the new authorities in our lives. Politics ruled most Americans' lives and thinking—where one could go, who one could see, what one could do. Not surprisingly, fear seemed to become the idol of American society. Surprisingly, fear also became an amazing stronghold and mindset in the lives of Christians. Against this growing backdrop of daily interwoven *new normal* fabric of our society and the quagmire of fear engulfing Christians, the Holy Spirit impressed each of us separately the vital role our FATHER held, how HE was either now being *pulled to the front* or *pushed to the back* like never before, depending upon who you were speaking to. Living became a barrage of questionable information, deception, confusion, distortions, and the weekly accumulative political beatings given and received from the media, governors, mayors, medical experts, police, and from you and me and everyone else. Overnight, the world turned into a swamp of masked talking heads. Our focus with the book moved from *creation* to FATHERLOVE.

Against this backdrop, we tried to remain focused enough to write a heart-, mind-, and *spirit*-transforming book!

Distractions and disruptions deeply affected individual groups like churches. To "dis" means *to undo something, to separate from.* So with this COVID di<u>s</u>ease…*society was being dissed.* <u>Dis</u>-*eased!* Society was being *separated from ease.* This began to put a damper on our journey. Still, we recognized it, and to overcome this *dis,* we deliberately prayed in faith to undo these adverse effects upon our time, life, and minds. Prayer works, and we received *"the mind of Christ."*

When we effectively overcame the *dis* darkness in the world around us, we returned to our motto: *"Converse…Write…Review… Repeat,"* and the words began flowing freely again.

Then the next shoe fell.

In spring, Duane was diagnosed with a profoundly serious and life-threatening cancer. A significant distraction as Duane was the lead writer! Especially in the middle of a worldwide pandemic! And therefore, a necessary delay in how we now would continue the writing. Of course, this required daily changes and readjustments in all our priorities.

Prayer and the voice of the Holy Spirit became the root and source of our lives. Duane is a research junky, so he effectively used this treatment period to research terms and topics discussed in the book. During seemingly unbearable pain and side effects of radiation and chemotherapy treatments, Duane began to write again. We pressed on, but somewhat more slowly and taking a slightly different twist.

Then some new revelation unfolded, and our discussions became more animated. The pace of writing began to increase.

Though the progress was continuing, there were some more temporary delays. Paul began to manifest some residual effects from two earlier health episodes concerning his heart and a hemorrhagic stroke. Additional delays occurred. But our faith is in our GOD, and we were guided by Holy Spirit.

Today, we're pleased to report that the book is finished through the Power of the Holy Spirit. Duane is pleased the Lord allowed him the Grace to see the work through to completion. FATHERLOVE has spread HIS GRACE over us and it is our prayer that you find this work to be anointed with the POWER of Holy Spirit and that it blesses you halve as much as it blessed us.

Praise the Lord!

With joy and rejoicing in the new anointing God has bestowed upon us, we finished to the glory of God! Please believe us when we say that the process of pressing on in faith and perseverance is worth everything. We could refer to it as "*the benefit*" we gained by the writing of this book! We have come to know in a new and deeper measure the reality and pleasure of a fresh knowing of His FATHERLOVE!

So why did we tell you "Our Story"?

So the glory of the Father and the reality of His life-giving *love*, will be restored in you also!

Our prayer is that you, the reader, will not only enjoy the style and message of the book but more so that you receive a revelation and transformation from it.

"Even so, come, Lord Jesus!"

CPSIA information can be obtained
at www.ICGtesting.com
Printed in the USA
LVHW020132210622
721684LV00001B/80

9 781639 613700